CONTENTS（目次）

JN113700

本書の構成と使い方

このワークブックは，APPLAUSE ENGLISH LOGIC AND EXPRESSION I の内容にしたがって作られています。教科書各課の Focus に出てくる文法事項の練習問題を，STEP 1 から 3 にかけて段階的に解いていく構成となっています。予習だけでなく，復習やテスト前の整理にも活用できます。各ページの内容は次のとおりです。

STEP 1 基本問題

文法項目ごとに，整序問題や英文和訳問題などを用意しています。

まずはこのステップで，それぞれの文法項目の基礎を確認しましょう。

STEP 2 実践問題

STEP 1 より少し難易度が上がった問題を用意しています。

さまざまな形式の問題を解いて，着実に文法項目を身につけましょう。

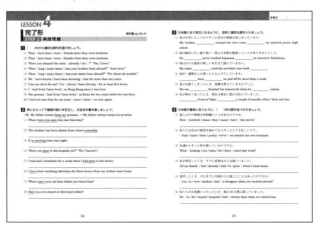

右の QR コードをタブレット端末で読み取ると，音声のウェブページに
つながります。次の URL からもアクセスできます。

https://www.kairyudo.co.jp/applause1lewb

STEP 3 まとめ問題

和文英訳問題など，英語でのライティングを練習できる問題が配置されています。
これまでに身につけた文法事項を用いてどこまで発信できるか確認しましょう。
また，教科書の各課 Model Dialog の音声を用いたディクテーション問題も用意しました。

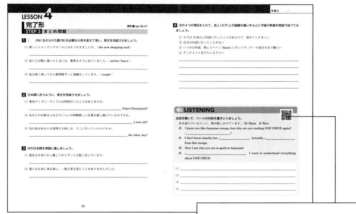

QR コード読み取り先より
音声を再生できます。

■1年の総合問題

1年間で学んだ文法事項を総復習するページです。3回に分かれた総合問題を解くことで，年
間をとおして学んだ内容の定着度を確認できます。

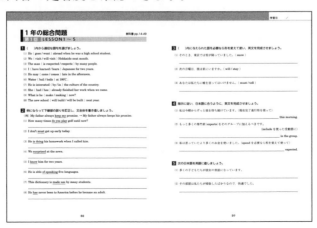

現在と過去を表す表現

STEP 1 基本問題

❶ 現在形

1 （　　）内の指示にしたがって書きかえましょう。

(1) I'm not busy on Saturdays. (I を We に変えて)

_____

(2) The students run very fast. (The students を The student に変えて)

_____

(3) We usually go to school by bus. (We を My brother に変えて)

_____

(4) You have some friends in London. (You を Lisa に変えて)

_____

2 次の英文を日本語に訳しましょう。

(1) I respect the leader of our band.

_____

(2) She teaches mathematics at high school.

_____

❷ 過去形

1 （　　）内の指示にしたがって書きかえましょう。

(1) His mother was at home. (His mother を His parents に変えて)

_____

(2) We play tennis every Sunday. (every Sunday を last Sunday に変えて)

_____

(3) I study English every day. (every day を yesterday に変えて)

_____

(4) We have a cute dog. (文末に ten years ago を加えて)

_____

2 次の英文を日本語に訳しましょう。

(1) A lot of foreigners came to Japan in those days.

_____

(2) I liked this song when I was a high school student.

_____

❸ 現在進行形

1　(　　　)内の指示にしたがって書きかえましょう。

(1) I am doing my homework now. (I を We に変えて)

_____

(2) He takes a walk in the park every morning. (every morning を now に変えて)

_____

(3) She swims in the pool every day. (every day を now に変えて)

_____

(4) My brother sometimes uses my computer. (sometimes を now に変えて)

_____

2　次の英文を日本語に訳しましょう。

(1) The children are sitting on the floor now.

_____

(2) Hurry up. Everybody is waiting for you.

_____

❹ 過去進行形

1　(　　　)内の指示にしたがって書きかえましょう。

(1) It is raining now. (now を at nine yesterday に変えて)

_____

(2) They are talking about the plan now. (now を then に変えて)

_____

(3) My mother is cooking in the kitchen. (文末に when I got home を加えて)

_____

(4) Tom was enjoying his dinner. (Tom を Tom and his wife に変えて)

_____

2　次の英文を日本語に訳しましょう。

(1) What were you looking for at that time?

_____

(2) I was watching television at seven this morning.

_____

現在と過去を表す表現

STEP 2 実践問題

1 ( )内から適切な語句を選びましょう。

(1) Columbus (discovers / discovered) America in 1492.

(2) Our school (has / is having) a large library.

(3) He usually listens to the radio, but at present he (watches / is watching) television.

(4) She (read / was reading) a book when I went into her room two hours ago.

(5) In Japan, people (take / are taking) their shoes off when they go into the house.

(6) Tom (put / puts) his coat on and left the room.

(7) What (do / does) your sister usually do after school?

(8) Mari and her brother (was / were) playing a video game.

(9) Our teacher (had / was having) long hair when he was young.

(10) I (lay / lied) on my back and looked up at the stars.

2 例にならって下線部の誤りを訂正し，文全体を書き直しましょう。

(例) My father always <u>keep my</u> promise. → My father always keeps his promise.

(1) One of my classmates <u>are</u> from Osaka.

_____

(2) The sun <u>rise from</u> the east.

_____

(3) I <u>do not study</u> hard when I was young.

_____

(4) We sat on the bank of the river and <u>talk</u> about our future.

_____

(5) <u>Do</u> the babies sleeping well now?

_____

(6) Where <u>were</u> your grandparents live in those days?

_____

(7) I <u>took</u> a bath when the doorbell rang.

_____

(8) Americans <u>are shaking hand</u> when they meet for the first time.

_____

3 日本語に合う英文になるように，空所に適切な語を入れましょう。

(1) 私の父は食後，皿を洗います。

My father ＿＿＿＿＿＿ the dishes ＿＿＿＿＿＿ meals.

(2) 彼女はそれについて何も言いませんでした。

She ＿＿＿＿＿＿ ＿＿＿＿＿＿ about it.

(3) 男子たちは今，砂浜に寝そべっています。

The boys ＿＿＿＿＿＿ ＿＿＿＿＿＿ on the sandy beach now.

(4) 昨日，私が見かけたとき，君はなぜ走っていたのですか。

Why ＿＿＿＿＿＿ you ＿＿＿＿＿＿ when I saw you yesterday?

(5) 昨日の午後，雨は降っていませんでした。

＿＿＿＿＿＿ ＿＿＿＿＿＿ raining yesterday afternoon.

(6) 彼は今，雑誌を読んでいます。

＿＿＿＿＿＿ ＿＿＿＿＿＿ a magazine now.

4 日本語の意味に合うように，(　　)内の語を並べかえましょう。

(1) ジョンソン氏はよく家族で中華料理を食べます。

Mr. Johnson (Chinese / often / dishes / eats) with his family.

＿＿＿＿＿＿＿＿＿＿＿＿＿＿＿＿＿＿＿＿＿＿＿＿＿＿＿＿＿＿＿＿

(2) スミス夫人は家で子どもたちにフランス語を教えました。

Mrs. Smith (French / her / taught / children) at home.

＿＿＿＿＿＿＿＿＿＿＿＿＿＿＿＿＿＿＿＿＿＿＿＿＿＿＿＿＿＿＿＿

(3) この学生たちはここでバスを待っているのですか。

(waiting / students / are / these) for the bus here?

＿＿＿＿＿＿＿＿＿＿＿＿＿＿＿＿＿＿＿＿＿＿＿＿＿＿＿＿＿＿＿＿

(4) 昨夜クリスは勉強している間に眠ってしまいました。

Last night (asleep / Chris / while / fell) he was studying.

＿＿＿＿＿＿＿＿＿＿＿＿＿＿＿＿＿＿＿＿＿＿＿＿＿＿＿＿＿＿＿＿

(5) 北海道はどちらのご出身ですか。

What part of (from / you / Hokkaido / are)?

＿＿＿＿＿＿＿＿＿＿＿＿＿＿＿＿＿＿＿＿＿＿＿＿＿＿＿＿＿＿＿＿

(6) 昨日の今頃は何をしていましたか。

(doing / you / what / were) at this time yesterday?

＿＿＿＿＿＿＿＿＿＿＿＿＿＿＿＿＿＿＿＿＿＿＿＿＿＿＿＿＿＿＿＿

LESSON

現在と過去を表す表現

STEP 3 まとめ問題

1 ( )内に与えられた語(句)を必要なら形を変えて使い，英文を完成させましょう。

(1) 私の祖父はイングランド出身です。(be / England)

_____

(2) 私たちの学校には広い講堂がありました。(a large auditorium)

_____

(3) 彼らは今，砂浜に寝そべっています。(lie / the beach)

_____

2 日本語に合うように，英文を完成させましょう。

(1) 彼女の兄は今朝，何も食べませんでした。

_____ this morning.

(2) 彼はふだん田舎に住んでいますが，今は東京で暮らしています。

_____, but

at present _____

(3) 私は勉強しているうちに眠ってしまいました。

_____ while _____

3 次の日本語を英語に直しましょう。

(1) 太陽は東から昇ります。

_____

(2) 昨日の今頃，私は宿題をしていました。

_____

4 次の5つの項目を入れて，自分のあこがれている人を英語で紹介しましょう。

① あこがれている人の名前　② その人の職業　③ その人がしていること・したこと

④ あこがれ始めた時期　⑤ その人の性格や特徴

_____

_____

_____

_____

_____

🔊 LISTENING

会話を聞いて，(1)〜(5)の内容を書きとりましょう。

本を読んでいるロンに，華が話しかけています。(H: Hana　R: Ron)

H:　Hi, Ron. (1)_____?

R:　I'm reading a book about Tezuka Osamu. (2)_____.

H:　I like his *manga*. I especially like *Black Jack*.

R:　Me too. (3)_____! I read *Astro Boy* when I was 10 years old.
　　And then (4)_____.

H:　You are very lucky! (5)_____, and now you are in Japan!

R:　Exactly! I love Japan.

(1) _____

(2) _____

(3) _____

(4) _____

(5) _____

LESSON 2

未来を表す表現

教科書 pp.20-25

STEP 1 基本問題

❶ 助動詞 will

1　日本語の意味に合うように( )内の語句を並べかえ，文全体を書き直しましょう。

(1) 来週は気温が上がると思います。

I think (rise / the temperature / will) next week.

_____

(2) 「ケンは入院しています」「え，本当ですか。それじゃあ，お見舞いに行きます」

"Ken is in hospital." "Oh, really? Then (visit / I'll / him)."

_____

2　次の英文を日本語に訳しましょう。

(1) You look very busy, so I won't stay long.

_____

(2) Don't worry. Your favorite team will win the game.

_____

❷ be going to

1　日本語の意味に合うように( )内の語句を並べかえ，文全体を書き直しましょう。

(1) 気をつけて。あなたはすべって転びそうです。

Be careful. You (to slip / are / going).

_____

(2) 「アンは入院しています」「ええ，知っています。明日お見舞いに行くつもりです」

"Anne is in hospital." "Yes, I know. (going / I'm / visit / to) her tomorrow."

_____

2　次の英文を日本語に訳しましょう。

(1) She looks very tired, so she's going to fall asleep.

_____

(2) He is going to ski in Nagano this winter, but his wife is against his plan.

_____

❸ 現在形

1　日本語の意味に合うように（　　）内の語句を並べかえ，文全体を書き直しましょう。

(1) 今度のクリスマスは日曜日にあたります。

Next Christmas (on / Sunday / falls).

_____

(2) 私の乗る飛行機は明日正午，ヒースロー空港に到着します。

My plane (at noon / at Heathrow / arrives) tomorrow.

_____

2　次の英文を日本語に訳しましょう。

(1) Your plane leaves at 5:00 a.m. tomorrow.

_____

(2) What time does the movie start tonight?

_____

❹ 進行形

1　日本語の意味に合うように（　　）内の語句を並べかえ，文全体を書き直しましょう。

(1) この夏バルセロナを訪問します。ホテルはすでに予約してあります。

(Barcelona / visiting / I'm) this summer. I've already booked a hotel.

_____

(2) 彼は明日，卒業式で送辞をすることになっています。

He (giving / is / a farewell speech) at the graduation ceremony tomorrow.

_____

2　次の英文を日本語に訳しましょう。

(1) I'm having dinner with Tom tonight.

_____

(2) Hurry up! Your train is leaving in a few minutes.

_____

LESSON 2

未来を表す表現

STEP 2 実践問題

1 ( )内から適切な語句を選びましょう。

(1) I think it (is / will be) fine the day after tomorrow.

(2) (It's going to / It will) rain soon. Look at those black clouds.

(3) A: What time is your train?

   B: My train (is going to leave / leaves) at 7:15 this evening.

(4) I'm (going to visit / visiting) Alex tomorrow. I have an appointment with him at 11:30.

(5) Your bag looks so heavy. I (am going to / will) carry it for you.

(6) A: Do you have any plans for this winter?

   B: (I'm going to / I will) ski in Hokkaido.

(7) A: Hey Tom, (I'll / I'm going to) go to the fireworks with Lisa tonight. Do you want to come?

   B: Sounds good. (I'll / I'm going to) see them with my sister, so (I'll / I'm going to) contact you around 7 o'clock.

(8) A: When will she come?

   B: Maybe she'll be here (for / in) a few minutes.

(9) A: Hurry up! They are leaving.

   B: Don't worry. They will wait for us (for / in) at least ten minutes.

2 例にならって下線部の誤りを訂正し，文全体を書き直しましょう。

(例) My father always keep my promise. → My father always keeps his promise.

(1) The weather forecast says it's cloudy this weekend.

_____

(2) My sister is going to be a doctor when she grow up.

_____

(3) "Do you want to see a movie tomorrow?" "I'll play tennis tomorrow."

_____

(4) "I'm going out for lunch. And you?" "Sounds good, then I'm going with you."

_____

(5) "Come downstairs. Dinner's ready." "I'm going."

_____

3 日本語に合う英文になるように，空所に適切な語を入れましょう。

(1) 彼の姉は来月 20 歳になります。

His sister ＿＿＿＿＿＿ ＿＿＿＿＿＿ twenty next month.

(2) 早く寝なさい。そうすれば風邪は引きません。

Go to bed early, ＿＿＿＿＿＿ you ＿＿＿＿＿＿ catch cold.

(3) 一時間後に私が伺います。

＿＿＿＿＿＿ be there ＿＿＿＿＿＿ an hour.

(4) 誰をパーティーに招くつもりですか。

Who ＿＿＿＿＿＿ you ＿＿＿＿＿＿ to invite to the party?

(5) 敵方はもう５点取りました。私たちはこの試合に負けそうです。

The other team already got five points. ＿＿＿＿＿＿ ＿＿＿＿＿＿ to lose this game.

(6) 彼女は今日，名古屋駅でいとこたちと会うことになっています。

＿＿＿＿＿＿ ＿＿＿＿＿＿ her cousins at Nagoya Station today.

4 日本語の意味に合うように，（　　）内の語句を並べかえましょう。

(1) その飛行機は明日の正午にロンドンへ向けて出発します。

The plane (at / for / leaves / noon / London) tomorrow.

＿＿＿＿＿＿＿＿＿＿＿＿＿＿＿＿＿＿＿＿＿＿＿＿

(2) 大阪行きの列車はまもなく出ます。

(is / Osaka / the train / leaving / for) soon.

＿＿＿＿＿＿＿＿＿＿＿＿＿＿＿＿＿＿＿＿＿＿＿＿

(3) 近い将来，大地震が起こるでしょう。

(a big earthquake / will / in / there / be) the near future.

＿＿＿＿＿＿＿＿＿＿＿＿＿＿＿＿＿＿＿＿＿＿＿＿

(4) 気分がよくありません。体調が悪くなりそうです。

I don't feel well. I think (sick / going / be / to / I'm).

＿＿＿＿＿＿＿＿＿＿＿＿＿＿＿＿＿＿＿＿＿＿＿＿

(5) 具合が悪そうですね。医者を呼んであげましょう。

You look sick. (a doctor / I / call / will / you).

＿＿＿＿＿＿＿＿＿＿＿＿＿＿＿＿＿＿＿＿＿＿＿＿

(6) この仕事は好きではないので，近々辞めるつもりです。

I don't like this job, so (soon / going / quit / I'm / to).

＿＿＿＿＿＿＿＿＿＿＿＿＿＿＿＿＿＿＿＿＿＿＿＿

LESSON 2
未来を表す表現
STEP 3 まとめ問題

1 （　　）内に与えられた語(句)を必要なら形を変えて使い, 英文を完成させましょう。

(1) どうか私に本当のことを言ってください。誰にも言いませんよ。(tell)

_____

(2) 弟は高校に入ったらハンドボール部に入るつもりでいます。(join / enter)

_____

(3) 彼女は明日, 卒業式でピアノを弾きます。(the graduation ceremony)

_____

2 日本語に合うように, 英文を完成させましょう。

(1) 彼はちっとも練習しません。次の試合は負けそうです。

He doesn't practice at all. _____

(2) 天気予報によると明後日は雨です。

The weather forecast says _____

(3) 私たちは半年後に結婚します。

_____ six months.

3 次の日本語を英語に直しましょう。

(1) その試験は明日の朝9時に始まります。

_____

(2) とても忙しそうですね。私がお手伝いしますよ。

_____

4 次の４つの項目を入れて，外国からきたお客さんと過ごす土曜日の予定を英語で発表しましょう。

① 横浜を案内する　　② 横浜の土曜日の天気は曇りのち晴れ

③ 横浜中華街(Yokohama Chinatown)に行って肉まん(meat buns)を食べる

④ 山下公園(Yamashita Park)と赤レンガ倉庫(Aka Renga)に行く

_____

_____

_____

_____

_____

🔊 LISTENING

会話を聞いて，(1)〜(5)の内容を書きとりましょう。

エイミーと拓は一緒に電車に乗っています。(*A*: Amy　*T*: Taku)

A:　Taku, (1)_____? Why do so many Japanese wear masks in spring?

T:　Well, (2)_____. They get runny noses, so they wear masks.

A:　That's too bad.

T:　(3)_____.

A:　The weather forecast says (4)_____, so (5)_____.

(1) _____

(2) _____

(3) _____

(4) _____

(5) _____

LESSON 3
助動詞
教科書 pp.28-33
STEP 1 基本問題

① can / could

1 日本語の意味に合うように( )内の語句を並べかえ，文全体を書き直しましょう。

(1) 姉はとても上手にギターを弾くことができますが，私はできません。

My sister (play / very well / the guitar / can), but I can't.

_____

(2) 「その知らせが本当ということはあるでしょうか」「ありえません」

"(true / can / be / the news) ?" "It can't be."

_____

(3) その少年が嘘をついているはずがありません。

The boy (telling / not / be / could) a lie.

_____

2 次の英文を日本語に訳しましょう。

(1) "Can I use your smartphone?" "Sorry, you can't."

_____

(2) "Could you show me the way to the station?" "Yes, of course."

_____

② may / might

1 日本語の意味に合うように( )内の語句を並べかえ，文全体を書き直しましょう。

(1) 本を借りる人は一度に3冊持ち出してよいです。

Borrowers (take out / at a time / may / three books).

_____

(2) あなたは間違っているかもしれないし，間違っていないかもしれません。

You (be / or / may / may not) wrong.

_____

2 次の英文を日本語に訳しましょう。

(1) "May I have dessert before dinner?" "Absolutely not!"

_____

(2) Bob is absent today. He might be sick.

_____

❸ must / should

1　日本語の意味に合うように（　　）内の語句を並べかえ，文全体を書き直しましょう。

(1) 子どもたちは暗くなる前に家に帰らなくてはなりません。

Children (before dark / must / home / go).

_____

(2) 彼女はそんなに長く歩いたあとで疲れているにちがいありません。

She (tired / be / after / must) such a long walk.

_____

(3) 彼はその小説家の作品を読むべきです。

He (of / read / should / the works) the novelist.

_____

2　次の英文を日本語に訳しましょう。

(1) You must not read my diary.

_____

(2) You should not waste your time.

_____

❹ be able to ～ / have to ～

1　日本語の意味に合うように（　　）内の語を並べかえ，文全体を書き直しましょう。

(1) アリスは明日までに宿題を終えることができるでしょう。

Alice (able / will / to / be) finish her homework by tomorrow.

_____

(2) 平日，兄は5時半に起床しなくてはなりません。

My brother (up / to / has / get) at 5:30 a.m. on weekdays.

_____

2　次の英文を日本語に訳しましょう。

(1) I was able to read the book in three hours.

_____

(2) He doesn't have to wait for me.

_____

LESSON 3
助動詞
STEP 2 実践問題

1 ( )内から適切な語句を選びましょう。

(1) The question was difficult, so I (can't / couldn't) answer it.

(2) You look pale. You (can't / should) go home now.

(3) I'll lend you my umbrella. It (won't / might) rain this afternoon.

(4) Julia won't talk to me. She (must / will) be angry with me.

(5) Alex (can't / could) be here in London. He moved to New York last month.

(6) In Japan, you (may / must) take off your shoes when you go into the house.

(7) You can borrow my car, but you'll (have to / must) bring it back before 10.

(8) You (don't have to / must not) break your promise.

(9) Usually I have to stand on the train but today I (had to / was able to) get a seat.

(10) "I feel terribly ill today."

"You (didn't have to / shouldn't) work so hard yesterday."

2 例にならって下線部の誤りを訂正し，文全体を書き直しましょう。

(例) My father always keep my promise. → My father always keeps his promise.

(1) I can read Chinese, but I can not speak it.

_____

(2) Don't believe him. He must not be telling the truth.

_____

(3) She can read when she was four.

_____

(4) His boss said that he may leave.

_____

(5) Soon people will able to go to the moon on holidays.

_____

(6) Last week my son had an accident and I must take him to the hospital.

_____

(7) Should I to take this medicine?

_____

(8) She has not to follow his advice.

_____

3 日本語に合う英文になるように，空所に適切な語を入れましょう。

(1) この包みはクリスマス当日まで開けてはいけません。

You ＿＿＿＿＿＿ open this parcel ＿＿＿＿＿＿ Christmas Day.

(2) 嘘をつくべきではありません。

You ＿＿＿＿＿＿ tell ＿＿＿＿＿＿.

(3) 一度や二度の失敗を気にする必要はありませんよ。

You ＿＿＿＿＿＿ ＿＿＿＿＿＿ to worry about a mistake or two.

(4) 駅までずっと歩かなくてはならなかったのですか。

＿＿＿＿＿＿ you ＿＿＿＿＿＿ to walk all the way to the station?

(5) 今日はとても忙しいですが，明日は買い物に行けるでしょう。

I'm pretty busy today, but ＿＿＿＿＿＿ ＿＿＿＿＿＿ able to go shopping tomorrow.

(6) カーテンの後ろに誰かいるにちがいありません。

＿＿＿＿＿＿ ＿＿＿＿＿＿ be someone behind the curtain.

4 日本語の意味に合うように，（　　　）内の語句を並べかえましょう。

(1) 私の代わりにこの荷物を二階に運んでもらえますか。

(upstairs / you / this baggage / carry / can) for me?

＿＿＿＿＿＿＿＿＿＿＿＿＿＿＿＿＿＿＿＿＿＿＿＿＿＿＿＿＿＿＿＿

(2) しばらく様子を見るべきでしょうか。

(a while / I / wait and see / for / should)?

＿＿＿＿＿＿＿＿＿＿＿＿＿＿＿＿＿＿＿＿＿＿＿＿＿＿＿＿＿＿＿＿

(3) あんな薄着だと彼女は風邪をひくかもしれません。

She (such light clothes / cold / catch / in / might).

＿＿＿＿＿＿＿＿＿＿＿＿＿＿＿＿＿＿＿＿＿＿＿＿＿＿＿＿＿＿＿＿

(4) キャンプ場を出るときにゴミを残してきてはいけません。

(your garbage / not / you / leave / must) behind when you leave the campground.

＿＿＿＿＿＿＿＿＿＿＿＿＿＿＿＿＿＿＿＿＿＿＿＿＿＿＿＿＿＿＿＿

(5) 彼は一晩中その痛みに耐えなくてはなりませんでした。

He (the pain / to / all night / put up with / had).

＿＿＿＿＿＿＿＿＿＿＿＿＿＿＿＿＿＿＿＿＿＿＿＿＿＿＿＿＿＿＿＿

(6) あなたは来月，帰国できないでしょう。

You (to your country / able / won't / to return / be) next month.

＿＿＿＿＿＿＿＿＿＿＿＿＿＿＿＿＿＿＿＿＿＿＿＿＿＿＿＿＿＿＿＿

LESSON 3
助動詞

STEP 3 まとめ問題

1 ( )内に与えられた語を必要なら形を変えて使い，英文を完成させましょう。

(1) 「この本を持って行ってもいいですか」「いいえ，駄目です」(take)

_____

(2) 「ここにいないといけませんか」「いいえ，その必要はありません」(stay)

_____

(3) そのチームは次の試合に勝つかもしれません。(win)

_____

2 日本語に合うように，英文を完成させましょう。

(1) 塩を取ってもらえませんか。

_____, please?

(2) お腹が空いているはずがありません。あなたはお昼を食べたばかりでしょう。

_____. You've just had lunch.

(3) 私はすぐ歯医者に行くべきでしょうか。

_____ immediately?

3 次の日本語を英語に直しましょう。

(1) あなたのお姉さんは入試に受かるにちがいありません。

_____

(2) 私たちは明日の朝早く家を出なくてはならないでしょう。

_____

4 次の４つの項目を入れて，富士山に登る外国人旅行者に注意事項を伝えましょう。

① それほど多くの食べ物と水を持って行く必要はない

② 山小屋 (the mountain huts) で食べ物と水を買うことができる

③ 山小屋で有料トイレ (paid toilets) を使うことができる

④ 自分のゴミは持ち帰らなくてはならない

_____

_____

_____

_____

_____

🔊 LISTENING

会話を聞いて，(1)〜(4)の内容を書きとりましょう。

　ロンと華が浅草を観光しています。(*R*: Ron　*H*: Hana)

R:　Wow! Look at the crowd. (1)_____.

H:　It surely is. This temple, Senso-ji, attracts a lot of foreign tourists as you see.

R:　Well, (2)_____. Can I look around the inside?

H:　Of course, you can. But (3)_____ when you go inside.

R:　Really? I didn't know that! (4)_____?

H:　With pleasure!

(1) _____

(2) _____

(3) _____

(4) _____

LESSON 4

完了形

STEP 1 基本問題

❶ 現在完了形

1 日本語の意味に合うように（　　）内の語を並べかえ，文全体を書き直しましょう。

(1) 私たちはすでにお昼ご飯を食べました。

We (had / already / have) lunch.

_____

(2) 夏は終わりました。

(passed / has / summer).

_____

(3) あなたは納豆をこれまでに食べたことはありますか。

Have (tried / ever / you) *natto*?

_____

(4) 私はその歌を2，3度聞いたことがあります。

I have heard that song (few / a / times).

_____

(5) 彼らは神戸に2年間住んでいます。

They have lived in Kobe (years / for / two).

_____

(6) 私は今朝からずっと空腹です。

I've (hungry / since / been) this morning.

_____

2 次の英文を日本語に訳しましょう。

(1) He has gone to the library.

_____

(2) He has just been to the convenience store.

_____

(3) How many times has he been to Hawaii?

_____

(4) How long has he been in Japan?

_____

❷ 現在完了進行形

1　日本語の意味に合うように（　　）内の語を並べかえ，文全体を書き直しましょう。

(1) 今日は朝からずっと雨が降っています。

It (been / raining / has) since this morning.

_____

(2) その子たちは少なくとも 10 時間眠り続けています。

The children (sleeping / been / have) for at least ten hours.

_____

2　次の英文を日本語に訳しましょう。

How long have you been studying Japanese?

_____

❸ 過去完了形

1　日本語の意味に合うように（　　）内の語を並べかえ，文全体を書き直しましょう。

(1) 父が帰って来たとき，私たちはちょうど夕食を終えたところでした。

We (just / finished / had) dinner when my father came home.

_____

(2) 祖父は亡くなる前に，何度もパリを訪れたことがありました。

My grandfather (visited / had / Paris) many times before he died.

_____

(3) 彼は神戸に引っ越す前に，数年間シドニーに住んでいました。

He (lived / had / in) Sydney for a couple of years before he moved to Kobe.

_____

2　次の英文を日本語に訳しましょう。

(1) When we got to the stadium, the game had already started.

_____

(2) I remembered that I had seen the lady before.

_____

(3) How long had you been a teacher when we first met?

_____

LESSON 4

完了形

STEP 2 実践問題

1 (   )内から適切な語句を選びましょう。

(1) They (have been / were) friends since they were students.

(2) They (have been / were) friends when they were students.

(3) "Have you cleaned the room (already / yet) ?" "Yes, I have."

(4) "How (long / many times) has your brother been abroad?" "Just twice."

(5) "How (long / many times) has your sister been abroad?" "For about six months."

(6) We (have known / have been knowing) him for more than ten years.

(7) Can you drive for me? I've (driven / been driving) for at least five hours.

(8) I (had lived / have lived) in Hong Kong since I was born.

(9) His parents (had lived / have lived) in Rome for two years before he was born.

(10) I had not seen him for six years (since / when) we met again.

2 例にならって下線部の誤りを訂正し，文全体を書き直しましょう。

(例) My father always keep my promise. → My father always keeps his promise.

(1) Where have you seen him last Saturday?

_____

(2) The student has been absent from school yesterday.

_____

(3) It is snowing since last night.

_____

(4) "Have you gone to the hospital yet?" "No, I haven't."

_____

(5) I had had a headache for a week when I had gone to the doctor.

_____

(6) I have been watching television for three hours when my mother came home.

_____

(7) Where have your cat been before you found him?

_____

(8) Had you ever stayed at this hotel before?

_____

3 日本語に合う英文になるように，空所に適切な語を入れましょう。

(1) 弟は中学に入ってからずっと自分の部屋を欲しがっています。

My brother ＿＿＿＿＿＿ wanted his own room ＿＿＿＿＿＿ he entered junior high school.

(2) 彼は横浜に引っ越す前に一度も日本語を勉強したことがありませんでした。

He ＿＿＿＿＿＿ never studied Japanese ＿＿＿＿＿＿ he moved to Yokohama.

(3) 妹はその小説家の新しい本をまだ読んでいません。

My sister ＿＿＿＿＿＿ read the novelist's new book ＿＿＿＿＿＿.

(4) 雨が一週間以上も降ったり止んだりしています。

＿＿＿＿＿＿ been ＿＿＿＿＿＿ on and off for more than a week.

(5) 息子は寝てしまったとき，宿題を終えていませんでした。

My son ＿＿＿＿＿＿ finished his homework when he ＿＿＿＿＿＿ asleep.

(6) 私が初めて会ったとき，彼女は東京に数か月住んでいました。

＿＿＿＿＿＿ lived in Tokyo ＿＿＿＿＿＿ a couple of months when I first met her.

4 日本語の意味に合うように，（　　）内の語を並べかえましょう。

(1) 彼らはその映画を何回観たことがあるのですか。

How (watched / times / they / many / have) the movie?

＿＿＿＿＿＿＿＿＿＿＿＿＿＿＿＿＿＿＿＿＿＿＿＿＿＿＿＿＿＿

(2) 私たちは自分の商売を始めてからずっととても忙しいです。

(busy / since / been / pretty / we've) we started our own business.

＿＿＿＿＿＿＿＿＿＿＿＿＿＿＿＿＿＿＿＿＿＿＿＿＿＿＿＿＿＿

(3) 先週からずっと何を探しているのですか。

What (looking / you / been / for / have) since last week?

＿＿＿＿＿＿＿＿＿＿＿＿＿＿＿＿＿＿＿＿＿＿＿＿＿＿＿＿＿＿

(4) 私が帰宅したとき，すでに家族はみんな寝ていました。

All my family (bed / already / had / to / gone) when I came home.

＿＿＿＿＿＿＿＿＿＿＿＿＿＿＿＿＿＿＿＿＿＿＿＿＿＿＿＿＿＿

(5) 留学したとき，それまでに外国の人と話したことはあったのですか。

(you / to / ever / spoken / had) a foreigner when you studied abroad?

＿＿＿＿＿＿＿＿＿＿＿＿＿＿＿＿＿＿＿＿＿＿＿＿＿＿＿＿＿＿

(6) 私たちがお見舞いに行ったとき，彼は20日間入院していました。

He (in / for / stayed / hospital / had) twenty days when we visited him.

＿＿＿＿＿＿＿＿＿＿＿＿＿＿＿＿＿＿＿＿＿＿＿＿＿＿＿＿＿＿

LESSON 4
完了形

教科書 pp.36-41

STEP 3 まとめ問題

1 ( )内に与えられた語(句)を必要なら形を変えて使い，英文を完成させましょう。

(1) 新しいショッピングモールにはもう行きましたか。(the new shopping mall)

_____

(2) 私たちが駅に着いたときには，電車はすでに出ていました。(arrive / leave)

_____

(3) 私は家に帰ってから数時間ずっと宿題をしています。(couple)

_____

2 日本語に合うように，英文を完成させましょう。

(1) 東京ディズニーランドには何回行ったことがありますか。

_____ Tokyo Disneyland?

(2) あなたのお姉さんはどのくらいの時間新しい仕事を探し続けているのですか。

_____ a new job?

(3) 先日私があなたを訪問する前には，どこに行っていたのですか。

_____ the other day?

3 次の日本語を英語に直しましょう。

(1) 彼女は日本に引っ越してからずっと大阪に住んでいます。

_____

(2) 彼らは日本に来る前に，一度も雪を見たことがありませんでした。

_____

26

4 次の４つの項目を入れて，友人（カズ）との経験の違いをもとに今後の希望を英語で述べてみましょう。

① カズは 10 回以上外国に行ったことがあるので，彼がうらやましい

② 自分は外国に行ったことがない

③ いつかは外国，特にスペイン（**Spain**）に行ってサッカーの試合を生で観たい

④ そこの人々と友だちになりたい

_____

_____

_____

_____

_____

🔊 LISTENING

会話を聞いて，(1)〜(4)の内容を書きとりましょう。

本を読んでいるロンに，華が話しかけています。（*H*: Hana　*R*: Ron）

H: I know you like Japanese *manga*, but why are you reading *ONE PIECE* again?
(1)_____?

R: I don't know exactly, but (2)_____. Actually, (3)_____ from this *manga*.

H: Now I see why you are so good at Japanese!

R: (4)_____. I want to understand everything about *ONE PIECE*.

(1) _____

(2) _____

(3) _____

(4) _____

LESSON 5
受動態

教科書 pp.44-49

STEP 1 基本問題

❶ 基本的な受動態

1　日本語の意味に合うように（　）内の語を並べかえ，文全体を書き直しましょう。

(1) あのパン屋ではイングリッシュ・マフィンが売られています。

English muffins (sold / at / are) that bakery.

_____

(2) そのウェブサイトは多くの人に閲覧されています。

The website (by / viewed / is) many people.

_____

(3) 大金が金庫から盗まれました。

A lot of money (stolen / from / was) the safe.

_____

2　次の英文を日本語に訳しましょう。

(1) Is English spoken in that country?

_____

(2) Were those pictures really painted by Banksy?

_____

❷ by 以外の前置詞を伴う受動態

1　日本語の意味に合うように（　）内の語を並べかえ，文全体を書き直しましょう。

(1) その試合で3人の選手が怪我をしました。

Three players (injured / in / were) the game.

_____

(2) 娘はプレゼントに満足しています。

My daughter (with / satisfied / is) the present.

_____

2　次の英文を日本語に訳しましょう。

(1) He was killed in the fire.

_____

(2) She was disappointed with the result of the test.

_____

❸ 群動詞を用いた受動態

1　日本語の意味に合うように（　　）内の語を並べかえ，文全体を書き直しましょう。

(1) マイクは今日クラスメイトに笑われました。

Mike was (at / by / laughed) his classmates today.

_____

(2) ダンスの先生は弟子たちに尊敬されています。

The dancing master is looked (to / by / up) his pupils.

_____

2　次の英文を日本語に訳しましょう。

(1) I was spoken to by a foreigner in Japanese.

_____

(2) The player is relied on by her teammates.

_____

❹ 助動詞を含む受動態

1　日本語の意味に合うように（　　）内の語を並べかえ，文全体を書き直しましょう。

(1) そのピアノコンクールは来年10月に開催されます。

The piano competition (held / will / be) in October next year.

_____

(2) 日中は星が見えません。

Stars (be / seen / can't) in the daytime.

_____

2　次の英文を日本語に訳しましょう。

(1) A full moon may be seen on the 21st this month.

_____

(2) This lesson should not be forgotten.

_____

LESSON 5

受動態

STEP 2 実践問題

1 各組の文がほぼ同じ意味になるように，空所に適切な語を入れましょう。

(1) a. About one million people visit this zoo every year.

b. This zoo ＿＿＿＿＿＿ ＿＿＿＿＿＿ ＿＿＿＿＿＿ about one million people every year.

(2) a. His mother took him to the hospital.

b. He ＿＿＿＿＿＿ ＿＿＿＿＿＿ ＿＿＿＿＿＿ the hospital by his mother.

(3) a. People made these machines in China.

b. These machines ＿＿＿＿＿＿ ＿＿＿＿＿＿ ＿＿＿＿＿＿ China.

(4) a. They sell vegetables at the store.

b. Vegetables ＿＿＿＿＿＿ ＿＿＿＿＿＿ ＿＿＿＿＿＿ the store.

(5) a. We call this flower *tampopo* in Japanese.

b. This flower ＿＿＿＿＿＿ ＿＿＿＿＿＿ ＿＿＿＿＿＿ in Japanese.

(6) a. The result of the exam satisfied their teacher.

b. Their teacher ＿＿＿＿＿＿ ＿＿＿＿＿＿ ＿＿＿＿＿＿ the results of the exam.

(7) a. Toyotomi Hideyoshi relied on Maeda Toshiie.

b. Maeda Toshiie ＿＿＿＿＿＿ relied ＿＿＿＿＿＿ ＿＿＿＿＿＿ Toyotomi Hideyoshi.

(8) a. All the students must follow the school rules.

b. The school rules must ＿＿＿＿＿＿ ＿＿＿＿＿＿ ＿＿＿＿＿＿ all the students.

2 例にならって下線部の誤りを訂正し，文全体を書き直しましょう。

（例）My father always <u>keep my</u> promise. → My father always keeps his promise.

(1) I was taught French <u>from</u> my mother.

＿＿＿＿＿＿＿＿＿＿＿＿＿＿＿＿＿＿＿＿＿＿＿＿＿＿＿＿＿＿＿＿

(2) Spanish is not spoken <u>by</u> the country.

＿＿＿＿＿＿＿＿＿＿＿＿＿＿＿＿＿＿＿＿＿＿＿＿＿＿＿＿＿＿＿＿

(3) I was <u>spoken</u> by an old woman in the park.

＿＿＿＿＿＿＿＿＿＿＿＿＿＿＿＿＿＿＿＿＿＿＿＿＿＿＿＿＿＿＿＿

(4) He seriously <u>injured</u> in the traffic accident.

＿＿＿＿＿＿＿＿＿＿＿＿＿＿＿＿＿＿＿＿＿＿＿＿＿＿＿＿＿＿＿＿

(5) <u>Do</u> these chairs made <u>in</u> plastic?

＿＿＿＿＿＿＿＿＿＿＿＿＿＿＿＿＿＿＿＿＿＿＿＿＿＿＿＿＿＿＿＿

(6) Will the work <u>is</u> finished by tomorrow?

＿＿＿＿＿＿＿＿＿＿＿＿＿＿＿＿＿＿＿＿＿＿＿＿＿＿＿＿＿＿＿＿

3 日本語に合う英文になるように，空所に適切な語を入れましょう。

(1) これらの身振りは現地の人々には使われません。

These gestures ＿＿＿＿＿＿ ＿＿＿＿＿＿ by local people.

(2) そのラグビーの試合はどのくらいの人々がテレビで見たのですか。

How many people ＿＿＿＿＿＿ the rugby game watched ＿＿＿＿＿＿ on TV?

(3) 多くの民間人がその戦争で亡くなりました。

A lot of civilians ＿＿＿＿＿＿ ＿＿＿＿＿＿ in the war.

(4) 私はその映画の結末にがっかりしています。

＿＿＿＿＿＿ ＿＿＿＿＿＿ with the ending of the movie.

(5) 来年カラオケ大会は開催されません。

The *karaoke* contest ＿＿＿＿＿＿ ＿＿＿＿＿＿ held next year.

(6) お年寄りは敬うべきです。

Old people should ＿＿＿＿＿＿ looked up ＿＿＿＿＿＿.

4 日本語の意味に合うように，（　　）内の語句を並べかえましょう。

(1) 私たちは毎年ピーターからクリスマスカードを送られています。

(a Christmas card / sent / by / are / we) Peter every year.

＿＿＿＿＿＿＿＿＿＿＿＿＿＿＿＿＿＿＿＿＿＿＿＿＿＿＿＿＿＿＿＿＿

(2) この食べ物はハギスといって，スコットランドではよく食べられています。

This food is (haggis / commonly eaten / called / is / and) in Scotland.

＿＿＿＿＿＿＿＿＿＿＿＿＿＿＿＿＿＿＿＿＿＿＿＿＿＿＿＿＿＿＿＿＿

(3) それらの寺院と神社が数百年前に建てられたのですか。

(shrines / built / and / were / those temples) several hundred years ago?

＿＿＿＿＿＿＿＿＿＿＿＿＿＿＿＿＿＿＿＿＿＿＿＿＿＿＿＿＿＿＿＿＿

(4) その鉄道事故で怪我をした人はごくわずかしかいませんでした。

(in / were / passengers / injured / very few) the railway accident.

＿＿＿＿＿＿＿＿＿＿＿＿＿＿＿＿＿＿＿＿＿＿＿＿＿＿＿＿＿＿＿＿＿

(5) あなたは明日，友だちに笑われるかもしれません。

You (by / be / at / may / laughed) your friends tomorrow.

＿＿＿＿＿＿＿＿＿＿＿＿＿＿＿＿＿＿＿＿＿＿＿＿＿＿＿＿＿＿＿＿＿

(6) 真面目なスピーチに冗談は入れるべきではありません。

Jokes (in / be / not / included / should) a serious speech.

＿＿＿＿＿＿＿＿＿＿＿＿＿＿＿＿＿＿＿＿＿＿＿＿＿＿＿＿＿＿＿＿＿

LESSON 5

受動態

STEP 3 まとめ問題

1 ( )内に与えられた語(句)を必要なら形を変えて使い，英文を完成させましょう。

(1) その書店に漫画は売っていません。(comic books / bookstore)

_____

(2) その交通事故で 4 人が怪我をしました。(injure)

_____

(3) そのキャプテンはチームメイトから尊敬されています。(look)

_____

2 日本語に合うように，英文を完成させましょう。

(1) 毎週末に父が夕食を作ります。

Dinner _____

(2) サポーターたちは試合の結果にがっかりするにちがいありません。

The supporters _____

(3) そのセールスマンを信頼することはできません。

The salesperson _____

3 次の日本語を英語に直しましょう。

(1) カナダには公用語が 2 つあります。英語とフランス語がそこでは話されています。

_____

(2) 私は今朝，知らない人に話しかけられました。

_____

4 次の 4 つの項目を入れて，お好み焼き (*okonomiyaki*) を英語で紹介しましょう。

① 日本のパンケーキ (**pancake**) の一種である

② 小麦粉，卵，キャベツ (**cabbage**) などから作られている

③ 大阪や広島で多くの人に食べられている

④ 安くておいしいから日本ではとても人気がある

_____

_____

_____

_____

_____

🔊 LISTENING

会話を聞いて，(1)～(4)の内容を書きとりましょう。

拓とエイミーはパンを見て話しています。(*T*: Taku *A*: Amy)

T: (1)_____. What is it, Amy?

A: It is called *rosetta* and is commonly eaten in Italy. (2)_____ at the Italian Fair yesterday. Then this morning, I tried to bake it myself.

T: I see. It looks good. Can I try some?

A: Sure! (3)_____.

T: Thank you. Wow! It's delicious. What is it made from?

A: (4)_____, sugar, and salt.

(1) _____

(2) _____

(3) _____

(4) _____

LESSON 6
比較①（比較級，最上級）

教科書 pp.52-57

STEP 1 基本問題

❶ 比較級を用いた表現

1 日本語の意味に合うように（　）内の語を並べかえ，文全体を書き直しましょう。

(1) この携帯電話はあの携帯電話より安価です。

This mobile phone (than / is / cheaper) that one.

_____

(2) デイビッドはあのアスリートより速く走れます。

David can (faster / run / than) that athlete.

_____

(3) クリケットはスリランカではサッカーより人気があります。

Cricket is (popular / than / more) soccer in Sri Lanka.

_____

2 次の英文を日本語に訳しましょう。

Her husband speaks English more slowly than she does.

_____

❷ 最上級を用いた表現

1 日本語の意味に合うように（　）内の語を並べかえ，文全体を書き直しましょう。

(1) オーストラリアは世界でもっとも小さい大陸です。

Australia is (the / continent / smallest) in the world.

_____

(2) 彼はチームの全メンバーの中でいちばん早く起床します。

He gets up (all / of / earliest / the) the members in the team.

_____

(3) これはこの店でもっとも高価な品です。

This is (expensive / the / most) item in this shop.

_____

2 次の英文を日本語に訳しましょう。

He carried the box most carefully of the three boys.

_____

❸ 不規則変化する比較級，最上級を用いた表現

1　日本語の意味に合うように（　　）内の語を並べかえ，文全体を書き直しましょう。

(1) 彼女は絵を描くのが彼女の先生より上手です。

She is (drawing / at / better) pictures than her teacher.

_____

(2) その国の経済はあなたの国の経済より悪いです。

The economy of the country is (than / that / worse) of your country.

_____

2　次の英文を日本語に訳しましょう。

(1) My brother cooks the best in my family.

_____

(2) He danced worst of all the members in his team.

_____

❹ 比較級，最上級を用いたさまざまな表現

1　日本語の意味に合うように（　　）内の語を並べかえ，文全体を書き直しましょう。

(1) 彼女は 3 年前よりずっと上手にピアノを弾きます。

She is a (much / pianist / better) than she was three years ago.

_____

(2) アメリカ合衆国は人口が世界で 3 番目に多いです。

The U.S.A has the (largest / population / third) in the world.

_____

2　次の英文を日本語に訳しましょう。

(1) The sooner you start, the sooner you can get there.

_____

(2) Picasso was one of the greatest artists in the 20th century.

_____

比較① （比較級，最上級）

STEP 2 実践問題

1 ( )内から適切な語句を選びましょう。

(1) This quiz is more (easy / difficult) than that one.

(2) This article is (more bad / worse) than the previous one.

(3) My mother looks (more old / younger) than she is.

(4) My brother goes to bed (earlier / more early) than I do.

(5) Your garden is more (beautiful / beautifully) than ours.

(6) I like winter best (in / of) the four seasons.

(7) In Japan, August is the hottest month (in / of) the year.

(8) Chris is (the more / the most) intelligent student in this university.

(9) (The more / The most) she practiced, the better she played.

(10) K2 is the second (higher / highest) mountain in the world.

(11) He is a (far / very) better cook than he was two years ago.

2 例にならって下線部の誤りを訂正し，文全体を書き直しましょう。

（例）My father always keep my promise. → My father always keeps his promise.

(1) My car is cheaper than you.

_____

(2) The tail of this dog is longer than my dog.

_____

(3) It is very hot today than yesterday.

_____

(4) He looks tired than he was last week.

_____

(5) Is he the most funny in all your friends?

_____

(6) The view from this building is the best beautiful in Tokyo.

_____

(7) Nero was one of the worst emperor in Roman history.

_____

(8) The more he studied history, the more he became interested in it.

_____

3 日本語に合う英文になるように，空所に適切な語を入れましょう。

(1) カリフォルニアの人口はカナダの人口より多いです。

The population of California is ＿＿＿＿＿＿ than ＿＿＿＿＿＿ of Canada.

(2) 彼はこのチームでいちばん人気がある選手です。

He is the ＿＿＿＿＿＿ ＿＿＿＿＿＿ player in this team.

(3) 彼の妻は彼より慎重に車を運転します。

His wife drives the car ＿＿＿＿＿＿ ＿＿＿＿＿＿ than he does.

(4) 今朝は昨日より早く家を出なくてはなりません。

I have to leave home ＿＿＿＿＿＿ this morning than I ＿＿＿＿＿＿ yesterday.

(5) どの種類の映画がいちばん好きですか。

What kind of movie do you like ＿＿＿＿＿＿ ＿＿＿＿＿＿?

(6) 年をとればとるほど，記憶力は弱くなります。

＿＿＿＿＿＿ ＿＿＿＿＿＿ we grow, the weaker our memory becomes.

4 日本語の意味に合うように，（　　）内の語を並べかえましょう。

(1) その歌手は5年前よりはるかに有名になりました。

The singer (famous / far / became / than / more) he was five years ago.

＿＿＿＿＿＿＿＿＿＿＿＿＿＿＿＿＿＿＿＿＿＿＿＿＿＿＿＿＿＿＿＿

(2) 先生たちは先週よりずっと忙しそうです。

The teachers look (than / were / busier / much / they) last week.

＿＿＿＿＿＿＿＿＿＿＿＿＿＿＿＿＿＿＿＿＿＿＿＿＿＿＿＿＿＿＿＿

(3) 私はジョンが知っている医者よりよい医者を知っています。

I know a (John / doctor / than / better / does).

＿＿＿＿＿＿＿＿＿＿＿＿＿＿＿＿＿＿＿＿＿＿＿＿＿＿＿＿＿＿＿＿

(4) スティーブはその質問にクラスでいちばん素早く答えました。

Steve answered (quickly / in / the / most / question) the class.

＿＿＿＿＿＿＿＿＿＿＿＿＿＿＿＿＿＿＿＿＿＿＿＿＿＿＿＿＿＿＿＿

(5) 北アメリカは6大陸の中で3番目に大きい大陸です。

North America (of / largest / the / is / third) the six continents.

＿＿＿＿＿＿＿＿＿＿＿＿＿＿＿＿＿＿＿＿＿＿＿＿＿＿＿＿＿＿＿＿

(6) ハリス氏はこの町で有数のお金持ちです。

Mr. Harris is (the / of / richest / one / men) in this town.

＿＿＿＿＿＿＿＿＿＿＿＿＿＿＿＿＿＿＿＿＿＿＿＿＿＿＿＿＿＿＿＿

LESSON 6
比較①（比較級，最上級）

教科書 pp.52-57

STEP 3 まとめ問題

1 （　　）内に与えられた語を必要なら形を変えて使い，英文を完成させましょう。

(1) 彼はピアノを彼の先生よりうまく弾きます。(well)

_____

(2) 高く登れば登るほど，ますます寒くなります。(high / cold)

_____

(3) これは京都でもっとも古いお寺の一つです。(temple)

_____

2 日本語に合うように，英文を完成させましょう。

(1) アフリカは6大陸の中で2番目に大きい大陸です。

Africa _____

(2) エレンは彼女の家族の中でいちばん慎重に運転します。

Ellen _____

(3) 彼は2年前よりもずっと上手に歌います。

_____two

years ago.

3 次の日本語を英語に直しましょう。

(1) 彼女はその三姉妹の中でいちばん年下です。

_____

(2) もっとゆっくり話していただけませんか。

_____

4 次の６つの項目を入れて，ギネスブックに載せるための企画を英語で発表しましょう。

① 企画名："The Biggest Daimonji"　② チーム名：the Giant Slayers

③ 来場者に参加を求め(ask visitors to join us)，世界一大きな「大」の人文字(human letter 'dai')を形成する(form)予定

④ 大という漢字(the Chinese character dai)の意味は「大きい」

⑤ 場所：校庭　⑥ 時期：文化祭中

_____
_____
_____
_____
_____
_____

🔊 LISTENING

会話を聞いて，(1)〜(4)の内容を書きとりましょう。

文化祭に向けて，拓が中庭で活動しています。(*A*: Amy　*T*: Taku)

A:　Wow! What are you doing?

T:　Hi, Amy. This is a part of the poster for our school festival.

A:　(1)_____! (2)_____?

T:　In fact, we want to be the Guinness World Record holders!

A:　Now I see! You are making (3)_____?

T:　Yes, (4)_____ at our school festival this year.

(1) _____
(2) _____
(3) _____
(4) _____

LESSON 7

比較② (同等比較，倍数比較)

教科書 pp.58-63

STEP 1 基本問題

❶ 同等比較

1　日本語の意味に合うように(　　)内の語を並べかえ，文全体を書き直しましょう。

(1) うちのネコは私の妹と同い年です。

Our cat (old / as / is / as) my sister.

_____

(2) 私の夫はあなたと同じくらいよくゴルフをします。

My husband plays (often / as / golf / as) you do.

_____

(3) 昨日は今日ほど暑くありませんでした。

Yesterday, (hot / wasn't / as / it) as today.

_____

2　次の英文を日本語に訳しましょう。

I cannot get up as early in the morning as my mother.

_____

❷ 倍数比較

1　日本語の意味に合うように(　　)内の語を並べかえ，文全体を書き直しましょう。

(1) この橋はあの橋の2倍の長さがあります。

This bridge is (as / twice / as / long) that one.

_____

(2) 東京の人口はあなたの国の人口の3倍です。

The population of Tokyo is (large / times / as / three) as that of your country.

_____

2　次の英文を日本語に訳しましょう。

(1) This sports car can go twice as fast as your car.

_____

(2) The earth is about four times as big as the moon.

_____

❸ 原級を用いたさまざまな比較表現

1　日本語の意味に合うように(　　)内の語を並べかえ，文全体を書き直しましょう。

(1) 私のクラスにはあなたのクラスと同じ人数の生徒がいます。

My class has (students / as / many / as) yours.

_____

(2) できるだけ早く戻ります。

I'll be back (possible / soon / as / as).

_____

2　次の英文を日本語に訳しましょう。

(1) He has as much money as you have.

_____

(2) My wife is as busy as ever.

_____

❹ 「世界一」を表すさまざまな比較表現

1　日本語の意味に合うように(　　)内の語を並べかえ，文全体を書き直しましょう。

(1) 東京スカイツリーは世界のほかのどの塔よりも高いです。

Tokyo Skytree is taller than (tower / other / in / any) the world.

_____

(2) 東京スカイツリーより高い塔は世界にありません。

(in / tower / other / no) the world is taller than Tokyo Skytree.

_____

(3) 琵琶湖ほど大きい湖は日本にありません。

No other lake in Japan (Lake Biwa / as / as / is / large).

_____

2　次の英文を日本語に訳しましょう。

(1) Nothing is as important as health.

_____

(2) Kaoru comes to school earlier than any other student in our school.

_____

LESSON 7

比較② （同等比較，倍数比較）

教科書 pp.58-63

STEP 2 実践問題

1 各組の文がほぼ同じ意味になるように，空所に適切な語を入れましょう。

(1) a. Wales is not as large as Scotland.

b. Wales is _____ _____ Scotland.

(2) a. My father doesn't look so old as he is.

b. My father looks _____ _____ he is.

(3) a. It is not as hot today as it was yesterday.

b. It is _____ today _____ it was yesterday.

(4) a. Jimmy plays the guitar better than Eric.

b. Eric _____ play the guitar as _____ as Jimmy.

(5) a. The TV program is not as interesting as it was last year.

b. The TV program is _____ interesting _____ it was last year.

(6) a. Her dog eats half as much food as mine.

b. My dog eats _____ as much food as _____ .

(7) a. We are sixteen, and our homeroom teacher is forty-eight.

b. Our homeroom teacher is _____ _____ as old as we are.

(8) a. Iron is the most useful of all metals.

b. Iron is more useful than _____ other _____ .

(9) a. The Nile is the longest river in the world.

b. _____ _____ river in the world is as long as the Nile.

(10) a. Time is more precious than anything else.

b. _____ is as precious as _____ .

2 例にならって下線部の誤りを訂正し，文全体を書き直しましょう。

(例) My father always keep my promise. → My father always keeps his promise.

(1) My cousin has games as many as you have.

_____

(2) My uncle drinks tea as many as an Englishman does.

_____

(3) This milk is not as fresh as that one.

_____

(4) Emma can run faster than any other boys in her class.

_____

3 日本語に合う英文になるように，空所に適切な語を入れましょう。

(1) 彼は妻と同じくらい慎重に車を運転しました。

He drove the car ＿＿＿＿＿ ＿＿＿＿＿ as his wife.

(2) そのアクション映画は私が気に入っている映画ほどおもしろくありません。

The action movie ＿＿＿＿＿ ＿＿＿＿＿ exciting as my favorite one.

(3) 彼女の部屋の広さは私の部屋の2倍です。

Her room is ＿＿＿＿＿ as large as ＿＿＿＿＿.

(4) 相変わらずまだ寒いです。

＿＿＿＿＿ is still as cold as ＿＿＿＿＿.

(5) できるだけ早く来てもらえますか。

Can you come as ＿＿＿＿＿ as ＿＿＿＿＿?

(6) ジョーダンほど高く跳べるバスケットボールプレーヤーは世界にいませんでした。

＿＿＿＿＿ ＿＿＿＿＿ basketball player in the world could jump as high as Jordan.

4 日本語の意味に合うように，（　）内の語を並べかえましょう。

(1) この新しいバッグはあの古いバッグと同じぐらい安価でした。

This new bag was as (that / cheap / old / as / one).

(2) ケビンは彼の兄ほど上手にピアノを弾くことはできません。

Kevin can't play (well / as / piano / as / the) his brother.

(3) 私の姉はあなたの5倍の数の本を持っています。

My sister has (books / times / many / as / five) as you.

(4) できるだけ多くの情報を手に入れるべきです。

You should get (possible / much / as / information / as).

(5) マーガレットは相変わらず熱心に数学を勉強しています。

Margaret is studying (ever / hard / mathematics / as / as).

(6) 彼はタイの他のどの俳優よりも人気があります。

He is (other / than / any / popular / more) actor in Thailand.

LESSON

比較② （同等比較，倍数比較）

教科書 pp.58-63

STEP 3 まとめ問題

1 （　　）内に与えられた語(句)を必要なら形を変えて使い，英文を完成させましょう。

(1) 私のデジカメはこのデジカメほど高価ではありません。(digital camera)

_____

(2) メキシコの人口は日本の人口とほぼ同じです。(Mexico / almost)

_____

(3) なるべく早く返信します。(reply)

_____

2 日本語に合うように，英文を完成させましょう。

(1) インドは日本の約 10 倍の大きさです。

India _____

(2) 私たちの学校にはあなた方の学校の 2 倍の数の生徒がいます。

Our school _____

(3) 当時エッフェル塔は世界でいちばん高い塔でした。

_____ the Eiffel

Tower in those days.

3 次の日本語を英語に直しましょう。

(1) 彼女は私の祖母と同じくらいゆっくりと歩きました。

_____

(2) 私は夏休みの間にできるだけ多くの本を読みたいです。

_____

4 次の４つの項目を入れて，食品ロスを減らすための意見を英語で述べてみましょう。

① 日本の人々は世界の人々が必要とする量の２倍の量の食品を無駄にしている

② 私たちが多くの食品を捨てるのはそれを食べ残すからである

③ これは大変深刻な問題なので，それについて何かすべきである

④ 私たちは自分が必要とする以上の食品を買うのを止めるべきだと私は思う

_____

_____

_____

_____

_____

🔊 LISTENING

会話を聞いて，(1)〜(4)の内容を書きとりましょう。

ロンと華が教室で一緒に昼食をとっています。(*R*: Ron   *H*: Hana)

R: (1)_____ except in *anime*!

H: A boxed lunch is called a *bento* in Japanese.

R: It looks like a full-course meal. And it is as colorful as a flower garden.

H: A Japanese *bento* (2)_____, you know.

R: To be honest, (3)_____. I want to make a nice boxed lunch like yours.

H: Really? Then, (4)_____, if you like.

(1) _____

(2) _____

(3) _____

(4) _____

LESSON 8

動名詞，to 不定詞①（名詞的用法） 教科書 pp.66-71

STEP 1 基本問題

❶ 動名詞の用法

1 日本語の意味に合うように（　　）内の語を並べかえ，文全体を書き直しましょう。

(1) 早起きは私には簡単です。

(early / is / up / getting) easy for me.

_____

(2) 彼のお気に入りの気晴らしは料理をすることです。

His favorite (cooking / pastime / is).

_____

(3) 私たちは教室を掃除し終わりました。

(finished / we / cleaning) our classroom.

_____

2 次の英文を日本語に訳しましょう。

When did you begin studying English?

_____

❷ 動名詞を用いたさまざまな表現

1 日本語の意味に合うように（　　）内の語を並べかえ，文全体を書き直しましょう。

(1) 拓也はギターを弾くのが得意です。

Takuya (at / good / is) playing the guitar.

_____

(2) 私たちはあなたからの連絡を楽しみにしています。

We (to / hearing / forward / look) from you.

_____

(3) 私は田舎暮らしには慣れています。

I (used / living / to / am) in the country.

_____

2 次の英文を日本語に訳しましょう。

Is Amy good at making friends?

_____

❸ to 不定詞の名詞的用法

1　日本語の意味に合うように(　　)内の語句を並べかえ，文全体を書き直しましょう。

(1) 毎日運動するのは私には難しいです。

(exercise / every day / is / to) difficult for me.

_____

(2) 彼の趣味はケーキをつくることです。

His hobby (make / is / cakes / to).

_____

(3) 私はカナダを訪れたいです。

I (visit / want / Canada / to).

_____

(4) 私の母は私にその椅子を運ぶように言いました。

My mother (carry / to / told /me) the chair.

_____

2　次の英文を日本語に訳しましょう。

Please ask him to call Mr. Sawada.

_____

❹ 形式主語，形式目的語を用いた表現

1　日本語の意味に合うように(　　)内の語を並べかえ，文全体を書き直しましょう。

(1) 彼女たちがそのルールを覚えるのは簡単です。

It is easy (them / remember / for / to) the rule.

_____

(2) 私をそこまで車で送ってくれるなんて，彼は親切ですね。

It is kind (to / him / drive / of) me there.

_____

(3) 私たちは新しい仕事を始めることは難しいとわかりました。

We found (it / start / difficult / to) a new job.

_____

2　次の英文を日本語に訳しましょう。

Is it dangerous for us to swim in the river?

_____

動名詞，to 不定詞① （名詞的用法） 教科書 pp.66-71

STEP 2 実践問題

1 （　　）内から適切な語句を選びましょう。

(1) (Watch / Watching) TV for many hours is not good for your eyes.

(2) We sometimes enjoy (to have / having) a conversation over coffee.

(3) Are you used to (make / making) anything with cardboard?

(4) She's looking forward to (join / joining) the band.

(5) I'm good at (playing / played) the violin.

(6) His favorite thing is (to eat / eats) something delicious.

(7) My sister decided (studying / to study) abroad.

(8) I want you (to show / show) me the way to the station.

(9) It is natural (of him / for him) (to get / get) angry.

(10) I think it impossible (to finish / finish) the task in time.

2 例にならって下線部の誤りを訂正し，文全体を書き直しましょう。

（例）My father always keep my promise. → My father always keeps his promise.

(1) Her dream is work for world peace.

_____

(2) I like run in the park before breakfast.

_____

(3) The driver practiced to park her car.

_____

(4) She is good at to teach math.

_____

(5) Thank you for invite me.

_____

(6) Kei hopes getting a new mobile phone.

_____

(7) It is important for us get enough rest.

_____

(8) I found it interesting listening to the expert's opinions.

_____

3 日本語に合う英文になるように，空所に適切な語を入れましょう。

(1) 辞書を使うことは生徒にとって有益です。

　　＿＿＿＿＿＿ a dictionary is helpful for students.

(2) 午後に雨が降り止みました。

　　It ＿＿＿＿＿＿ ＿＿＿＿＿＿ in the afternoon.

(3) 私は人前で話すことに慣れていません。

　　I'm not used ＿＿＿＿＿＿ ＿＿＿＿＿＿ in public.

(4) 私の父は小包を送ったことを忘れました。

　　My father forgot ＿＿＿＿＿＿ the package.

(5) 彼の仕事は地図をつくることです。

　　His work is ＿＿＿＿＿＿ ＿＿＿＿＿＿ maps.

(6) バッグを電車に置き忘れるとは，彼は不注意でした。

　　It was careless ＿＿＿＿＿＿ him ＿＿＿＿＿＿ leave his bag in the train.

4 日本語の意味に合うように，（　　）内の語を並べかえましょう。

(1) 日本での滞在を楽しみましたか。

　　(enjoy / in / you / staying / did) Japan?

　　＿＿＿＿＿＿＿＿＿＿＿＿＿＿＿＿＿＿＿＿＿＿＿＿＿＿＿＿

(2) 忘れずに宿題をやりなさい。

　　(your / to / remember / homework / do).

　　＿＿＿＿＿＿＿＿＿＿＿＿＿＿＿＿＿＿＿＿＿＿＿＿＿＿＿＿

(3) あなたは外国文化について学ぶことに興味がありますか。

　　(in / learning / are / interested / you) about foreign cultures?

　　＿＿＿＿＿＿＿＿＿＿＿＿＿＿＿＿＿＿＿＿＿＿＿＿＿＿＿＿

(4) あなたは将来，何になりたいですか。

　　What (to / you / want / do / be) in the future?

　　＿＿＿＿＿＿＿＿＿＿＿＿＿＿＿＿＿＿＿＿＿＿＿＿＿＿＿＿

(5) あなたが彼女のオフィスを見つけるのは簡単でしたか。

　　(to / easy / it / you / for / was) find her office?

　　＿＿＿＿＿＿＿＿＿＿＿＿＿＿＿＿＿＿＿＿＿＿＿＿＿＿＿＿

(6) 私はいちばんよい選択肢を選ぶのは難しいとわかりました。

　　I (hard / choose / it / found / to) the best option.

　　＿＿＿＿＿＿＿＿＿＿＿＿＿＿＿＿＿＿＿＿＿＿＿＿＿＿＿＿

LESSON 8

動名詞，to 不定詞① （名詞的用法） 教科書 pp.66-71

STEP 3 まとめ問題

1 （　　）内に与えられた語(句)を必要なら形を変えて使い，英文を完成させましょう。

(1) 私はたくさんの手紙を書き終えることはできません。(finish / write)

_____

(2) 彼は英語の歌を歌うのが得意になりたいです。(want / be good at)

_____

(3) 彼女はよく自分のスマートフォンを持っていくのを忘れます。(forget / take)

_____

2 日本語に合うように，英文を完成させましょう。

(1) 私の夢は京都でいくつかのお寺を訪れることです。

_____ in Kyoto.

(2) 母は私に毎日，花に水をあげるように言いました。

_____ some water every day.

(3) 私たちが災害のための準備をすることは重要です。

_____ for disasters.

3 次の日本語を英語に直しましょう。

(1) 私たち全員がその猫を助けようとしました。

_____

(2) 多くの人が，避難所への行き方を知っている必要があるとわかりました。

_____

4 次の 4 つの項目を入れて，日本滞在中の外国の人に台風への備えを英語で伝えましょう。

① 台風が予報される前にすべきことは 2 つ

② 防災マップ (a disaster prevention map) を入手して避難所への行き方を知る

③ 防災袋 (an emergency bag) を用意して中身 (the items you put in it) をチェックする

④ 備えあれば憂いなし (Providing is preventing)

_____

_____

_____

_____

_____

🔊 LISTENING

会話を聞いて，(1)〜(4)の内容を書きとりましょう。

防災の日に，拓とエイミーが避難所で見つけた段ボールについて話をしています。

(*T*: Taku　*A*: Amy)

T:　Do you know that cardboard is very useful at an emergency shelter?

A:　Is that so? But how do we use cardboard?

T:　For example, we can make beds, toilets, and partition screens

　　　(1)_____.

A:　That's very interesting. (2)_____ in case of an emergency.

T:　OK! (3)_____ at the community center this Sunday?

A:　That sounds good! (4)_____.

(1) _____

(2) _____

(3) _____

(4) _____

to 不定詞② (形容詞的用法, 副詞的用法) 教科書 pp.74-79

STEP 1 基本問題

❶ to 不定詞の形容詞的用法

1 日本語の意味に合うように(　　)内の語を並べかえ，文全体を書き直しましょう。

(1) 私は何か温かい飲み物がほしいです。

I want (to / something / drink / hot).

_____

(2) 彼には助けてくれる友だちがいませんでした。

He had (him / help / no / to / friend).

_____

2 次の英文を日本語に訳しましょう。

She has many pictures to show us.

_____

❷ to 不定詞の副詞的用法

1 日本語の意味に合うように(　　)内の語句を並べかえ，文全体を書き直しましょう。

(1) 私たちはテニスをするために公園に行きました。

We went to the park (play / to / tennis).

_____

(2) 私たちの父は80歳まで生きました。

Our father (to / lived / be) 80 years old.

_____

(3) 私はその知らせを聞いてうれしいです。

I'm happy (the news / hear / to).

_____

2 次の英文を日本語に訳しましょう。

(1) He went to the bookstore to buy a dictionary.

_____

(2) She grew up to be a famous writer.

_____

(3) I'm glad to see you again.

_____

❸ to 不定詞の否定形

1　日本語の意味に合うように（　　）内の語を並べかえ，文全体を書き直しましょう。

(1) 私の担当医は私に食べ過ぎないようにと言いました。

My doctor told (not / me / eat / to) too much.

_____

(2) 授業中にクラスメイトと話をしないことは重要です。

It is important (with / not / talk / to) your classmates during class.

_____

2　次の英文を日本語に訳しましょう。

My mother told us not to stay up late.

_____

❹ to 不定詞を用いたさまざまな表現

1　日本語の意味に合うように（　　）内の語を並べかえ，文全体を書き直しましょう。

(1) 私の弟は若すぎて，その仕事を受けられません。

My brother is (to / young / take / too) that job.

_____

(2) 彼女は車を数台持てるほどのお金持ちです。

She is (enough / have / to / rich) a few cars.

_____

(3) 私たちは時間に間に合うように早く出発しました。

We left early (to / in / be / order) in time.

_____

(4) 駅へはどのように行けばよいか教えていただけますか。

Could you tell me (to / get / how) to the station?

_____

2　次の英文を日本語に訳しましょう。

It was too hot to go out yesterday.

_____

to 不定詞② (形容詞的用法, 副詞的用法) 教科書 pp.74-79

STEP 2 実践問題

1 ( )内から適切な語句を選びましょう。

(1) Hokkaido has many places (visit / to visit).

(2) Do you have anything (to do / doing) today?

(3) I went to the library (borrowing / to borrow) a book.

(4) We are surprised (to see / seeing) our teacher here.

(5) My mother told me (not come / not to come) home too late.

(6) Many students use a bicycle (going / to go) to school.

(7) He is (too busy to take / busy too to take) part in the event.

(8) My sister is (enough old to / old enough to) go shopping alone.

(9) Be careful (to avoid in order / in order to avoid) accidents.

(10) I don't know (to do what / what to do).

2 例にならって下線部の誤りを訂正し，文全体を書き直しましょう。

(例) My father always <u>keep my</u> promise. → My father always keeps his promise.

(1) She left work early <u>see</u> a dentist.

_____

(2) I had no time <u>having</u> lunch today.

_____

(3) Would you ask him <u>not bother</u> us?

_____

(4) What did he come to Japan <u>doing</u>?

_____

(5) Is it better for us not <u>climbing</u> a mountain during winter?

_____

(6) We took a taxi <u>not in order to miss</u> the train.

_____

(7) He is <u>enough clever not repeat</u> the same mistake.

_____

(8) Please tell me <u>when leave</u>.

_____

3 日本語に合う英文になるように，空所に適切な語を入れましょう。

(1) 私はサインを書くためのペンがありません。

I have no pens ＿＿＿＿＿ ＿＿＿＿＿ my signature with.

(2) 会議の準備を手伝えず，申し訳ないと思います。

I'm sorry ＿＿＿＿＿ ＿＿＿＿＿ help prepare for the meeting.

(3) 私は普段，情報収集のためにパソコンを使います。

I usually use my PC ＿＿＿＿＿ ＿＿＿＿＿ ＿＿＿＿＿ gather information.

(4) 人が多すぎて，ステージの演技が見えません。

There are ＿＿＿＿＿ many people ＿＿＿＿＿ see the performance on the stage.

(5) その箱は私がひとりで運べるほど小さいです。

The box is small ＿＿＿＿＿ for me ＿＿＿＿＿ carry by myself.

(6) 私は彼にチケットを買うにはどこに行けばよいかを教えました。

I told him ＿＿＿＿＿ ＿＿＿＿＿ go ＿＿＿＿＿ buy a ticket.

4 日本語の意味に合うように，（　　）内の語句を並べかえましょう。

(1) 彼女は挑戦したいことがたくさんあります。

She has many (she / things / try / wants / to).

＿＿＿＿＿＿＿＿＿＿＿＿＿＿＿＿＿＿＿＿＿＿＿＿＿＿＿＿＿

(2) 彼女はケビンを見送るために空港に行きました。

She (the airport / see / to / went / to) Kevin off.

＿＿＿＿＿＿＿＿＿＿＿＿＿＿＿＿＿＿＿＿＿＿＿＿＿＿＿＿＿

(3) あなたにとって長時間，何もしないのはつらいですか。

Is it hard (do / you / not / anything / to / for) for many hours?

＿＿＿＿＿＿＿＿＿＿＿＿＿＿＿＿＿＿＿＿＿＿＿＿＿＿＿＿＿

(4) 彼らはよく戦ったが，その結果，その試合に負けました。

They (lose / only / the game / played well / to).

＿＿＿＿＿＿＿＿＿＿＿＿＿＿＿＿＿＿＿＿＿＿＿＿＿＿＿＿＿

(5) そのスープは私には熱すぎて，飲むことができません。

The soup is (me / drink / to / hot / for / too).

＿＿＿＿＿＿＿＿＿＿＿＿＿＿＿＿＿＿＿＿＿＿＿＿＿＿＿＿＿

(6) 私はそこに到着するにはどちらのルートを取るべきかわかりません。

I don't know (take / to / which / arrive / to / route) there.

＿＿＿＿＿＿＿＿＿＿＿＿＿＿＿＿＿＿＿＿＿＿＿＿＿＿＿＿＿

LESSON 9

to 不定詞② (形容詞的用法, 副詞的用法) 教科書 pp.74-79

STEP 3 まとめ問題

1 ( )内に与えられた語(句)を必要なら形を変えて使い, 英文を完成させましょう。

(1) 私は海外旅行をするために英語を勉強します。(travel abroad)

_____

(2) その映画は再び見てしまうほど素晴らしいです。(good / watch)

_____

(3) ケンは疲れすぎて, 夕食をつくることができませんでした。(tired / make)

_____

2 日本語に合うように, 英文を完成させましょう。

(1) 私はハエを追い払う道具を買うためにその店に行きました。

_____ a tool _____ flies.

(2) 彼はその問題に関する記事を読んで, 驚きました。

_____ an article about the issue.

(3) 彼女が本当のことを言わないのは当然です。

It is natural _____ the truth.

3 次の日本語を英語に直しましょう。

(1) 彼女は私と話すために立ち止まりました。

_____

(2) 私はワインのつくり方を学びたいです。

_____

4 次の5つの項目を入れて，留学先にお土産として持って行く風呂敷を英語で紹介しましょう。

① この四角い布（this square cloth）は風呂敷と呼ばれている

② 物を包み運ぶための伝統的な道具である

③ 日常生活で弁当箱を包むために使える

④ 買い物をするときはエコバッグ（an eco-friendly bag）として使える

⑤ 非常時にも役立つ

_____

_____

_____

_____

_____

🔊 LISTENING

会話を聞いて，(1)〜(4)の内容を書きとりましょう。

エイミーがハエに気をとられるロンを気にかけています。（*R*: Ron　*A*: Amy）

R: Oh! It bothers me a lot. Ahhhh!

A: (1)_____, Ron?

R: Well, it's a fly! It's flying around my *takoyaki*.

A: Just scare it away.

R: I hate it. Can you make a noise (2)_____?

A: No! I hate bugs. But, (3)_____, I saw an interesting ad on
the Internet the other day. (4)_____.

R: Really? Please show me the ad.

A: Sure. Let me see. Here it is.

(1) _____

(2) _____

(3) _____

(4) _____

LESSON 10

分詞

STEP 1 基本問題

❶ 前から修飾する分詞

1 日本語の意味に合うように（　　）内の語句を並べかえ，文全体を書き直しましょう。

(1) 彼女の眠っている赤ん坊は幸せそうです。

(baby / her / sleeping) looks happy.

_____

(2) その家の閉まった窓を開けることができますか。

Can you open the (in / windows / the house / closed)?

_____

2 次の英文を日本語に訳しましょう。

(1) We could listen to her interesting speech.

_____

(2) Who repaired the broken chair?

_____

❷ 後ろから修飾する分詞

1 日本語の意味に合うように（　　）内の語句を並べかえ，文全体を書き直しましょう。

(1) 向こうで泳いでいる少年がたけしです。

(over there / swimming / the boy) is Takeshi.

_____

(2) これが私たちの会社が建てたビルです。

This is (built / a building / our company / by).

_____

2 次の英文を日本語に訳しましょう。

(1) I talked to the man sitting next to me.

_____

(2) What is the language spoken in the country?

_____

(3) This is a shirt made in Italy.

_____

❸ 補語になる分詞

1　日本語の意味に合うように（　　）内の語句を並べかえ，文全体を書き直しましょう。

(1) 彼は2時間，立ったままでした。

　He (for / standing / two hours / remained).

_____

(2) 私はドアを鍵がかかったままにしておきました。

　I (locked / the door / kept).

_____

2　次の英文を日本語に訳しましょう。

(1) The fact remained unknown to many people.

_____

(2) Don't leave the water running.

_____

❹ 知覚動詞＋目的語＋補語（現在分詞）

1　日本語の意味に合うように（　　）内の語句を並べかえ，文全体を書き直しましょう。

(1) 私は彼が誰かに電話しているのを見ました。

　I (calling / saw / someone / him).

_____

(2) 私たちは彼女が隣の部屋で笑っているのを聞きました。

　We (her / heard / laughing) in the next room.

_____

(3) 私の母は建物が揺れているのを感じました。

　My mother (the building / shaking / felt).

_____

2　次の英文を日本語に訳しましょう。

(1) Did you see them entering the room?

_____

(2) I have heard her speaking French.

_____

LESSON 10
分詞

STEP 2 実践問題

1 ( )内から適切な語を選びましょう。

(1) Many (exciting / excited) fans rushed to the stage.

(2) It is very (boring / bored) work.

(3) He has a car (making / made) in America.

(4) The children (surrounding / surrounded) the dog are my students.

(5) There are many people (visiting / visited) my city as tourists.

(6) This is a picture (taking / taken) with Tim.

(7) I stood here (waiting / waited) for her to come.

(8) This product seems (damaging / damaged) to the environment.

(9) We found our old school (destroying / destroyed).

(10) I saw him (to apologize / apologizing) to someone.

2 例にならって下線部の誤りを訂正し，文全体を書き直しましょう。

(例) My father always <u>keep my</u> promise. → My father always keeps his promise.

(1) It is a <u>surprised</u> fact.

_____

(2) All of us removed the <u>falling</u> leaves.

_____

(3) No one lives in <u>the house burning</u>.

_____

(4) We know <u>the wearing glasses girl</u>.

_____

(5) This is a machine <u>designing</u> to work faster.

_____

(6) She showed a <u>satisfying</u> look.

_____

(7) You must keep the machine <u>run</u>.

_____

(8) I heard my name <u>calling</u> by someone.

_____

3 日本語に合う英文になるように，空所に適切な語を入れましょう。

(1) 英語で書かれたその手紙を読んでもらえますか。

Please read the letter _____ _____ English.

(2) 彼がそこで起きている物事を説明しました。

He explained the thing _____ _____.

(3) こちらが，あなたが予約した席です。

This is the seat _____ _____ you.

(4) 彼女は真夜中まで宿題をし続けました。

She _____ _____ her homework until midnight.

(5) 彼は疲労を感じ，早く就寝しました。

He _____ _____ and went to bed early.

(6) 私は彼女が彼のことを間違えて太郎と呼んでいるのを見ました。

I saw _____ _____ him Taro by mistake.

4 日本語の意味に合うように，(　　)内の語句を並べかえましょう。

(1) 私は私たちに手を振っている女性を知りません。

I (the woman / know / her hand / don't / waving) at us.

_____

(2) 私たちはその会社で印刷されたカレンダーを販売したいです。

We want to (by / sell / printed / the company / calendars).

_____

(3) ２台の車をつないでいるロープは非常に丈夫だ。

The (rope / two / connecting / is / cars / the) very strong.

_____

(4) 動物の絵が描かれたバスを見てください。

Look at (with / of / the bus / painted / animals / pictures).

_____

(5) 私は部屋の隅に置かれている小さな箱を見つけました。

I (placed / the corner / a small box / at / found) of the room.

_____

(6) 私はその日早くに彼が家を出ていくところをじっと見ていました。

I (him / early / watched / his house / leaving) on that day.

_____

LESSON 10
分詞
STEP 3 まとめ問題

1 (　　)内に与えられた語を必要なら形を変えて使い，英文を完成させましょう。

(1) 私は自分に仕事を提供するという E メールを受け取りました。(receive / offer)

_____

(2) それは私の家から盗まれた物です。(steal)

_____

(3) 彼女はその会社で働くことに興味を持ちました。(become / interest)

_____

2 日本語に合うように，英文を完成させましょう。

(1) 多くの種類のスマートフォンを開発するわが社は有名ではありません。

Our company _____ is not famous.

(2) 事故で負傷した男性が病院に運ばれました。

_____ was taken to the hospital.

(3) 彼女は彼らを雨の中で待たせたままにしておきました。

_____ in the rain.

3 次の日本語を英語に直しましょう。

(1) 彼女は私たちに勇気づける手紙をくれました。

_____

(2) 状況は長い間，変わらないままでした。

_____

4 次の会話を英語で書いてみましょう。

A: 男の子たちが野球をしているのが見えますか。

B: はい，見えます。

A: 彼らの一人が折れたバットを持っているのが見えます。たぶんほかの男の子たちに謝っています。彼を知っていますか。

B: 赤い帽子をかぶっている男の子のことを言っているのですか(Do you mean ～ ?)。

A: はい。

B: 彼は私のクラスメートの一人，ショウヘイ(Shohei)です。

_____

_____

_____

_____

_____

_____

_____

🔊 LISTENING

会話を聞いて，(1)～(4)の内容を書きとりましょう。

拓とロンが昨日の出来事について話をしています。(*T*: Taku　*R*: Ron)

T: Hey Ron! What's up? Is everything going well?

R: Pretty good!

T: Yes, I can tell! (1)_____.

R: What are you talking about?

T: Yesterday (2)_____. Who was she? I couldn't see her well.

R: Well, Taku. You know her very well! Last week
　　(3)_____ at lunch time.

T: No kidding! Was that Hana? (4)_____.

(1) _____

(2) _____

(3) _____

(4) _____

関係詞① （関係代名詞）

教科書 pp.88-93

STEP 1 基本問題

❶ 主格の関係代名詞

1 日本語の意味に合うように（　　）内の語句を並べかえ，文全体を書き直しましょう。

(1) 彼女にはオーストラリアに住んでいる友人がいます。

She has a friend (lives / Australia / who / in).

_____

(2) ３月の後の月は４月です。

The month (after / which / March / comes) is April.

_____

(3) 私は英語で書かれた手紙を読みました。

I read a letter (was / in English / written / that).

_____

2 次の英文を日本語に訳しましょう。

Can you see the house that has a beautiful garden?

_____

❷ 目的格の関係代名詞

1 日本語の意味に合うように（　　）内の語を並べかえ，文全体を書き直しましょう。

(1) 彼女が結婚した男性は看護師です。

The man (she / whom / married) is a nurse.

_____

(2) これが，私が昨日買ったいすです。

This is the chair (I / yesterday / bought / which).

_____

(3) 私が昨日見た映画は退屈でした。

The movie (yesterday / saw / that / I) was boring.

_____

2 次の英文を日本語に訳しましょう。

The woman who you met at the party is my sister.

_____

❸ 関係代名詞 what

1 日本語の意味に合うように（　　）内の語を並べかえ，文全体を書き直しましょう。

(1) 私たちが必要とするのはそのデータです。

(we / what / need) is the data.

_____

(2) それはあなたが昨日言ったことです。

That is (what / yesterday / said / you).

_____

(3) 私は彼が私に話したことを信じます。

I believe (me / he / what / told).

_____

2 次の英文を日本語に訳しましょう。

(1) He is not what he was.

_____

(2) I will send you what you want.

_____

❹ 関係代名詞の非制限用法

1 日本語の意味に合うように（　　）内の語句を並べかえ，文全体を書き直しましょう。

(1) 私には兄がいて，兄はライターとして活動しています。

I have a brother, (a writer / works / as / who).

_____

(2) 彼女は私にその DVD を貸してくれましたが，おもしろくなかったです。

She lent me the DVD, (was / which / interesting / not).

_____

2 次の英文を日本語に訳しましょう。

(1) She has two sons, who go to the same high school.

_____

(2) He has an expensive suit, which was made in Italy.

_____

関係詞① （関係代名詞）

教科書 pp.88-93

STEP 2 実践問題

1 (   )内から適切な語を選びましょう。

(1) The bus (who / which) goes to Osaka leaves at nine.

(2) Look at the boy (who / which) has long hair.

(3) This is a map (who / that) shows the way to the station.

(4) She is a teacher (whom / which) I respect.

(5) The car (whom / which) he bought recently was big.

(6) The camera (who / that) she showed me was expensive.

(7) She answered (which / what) I wanted to ask her.

(8) What is the thing (which / what) you are looking for?

(9) She will marry Mike, (whom / which) she has known for many years.

(10) He passed the exam, (who / which) nobody knows.

2 例にならって下線部の誤りを訂正し，文全体を書き直しましょう。

（例）My father always <u>keep my</u> promise. → My father always keeps his promise.

(1) English is a language <u>who</u> is spoken in many countries.

_____

(2) The people <u>which</u> live here are very kind.

_____

(3) This is the pen <u>whom</u> the author wrote the novel with.

_____

(4) He's the person <u>which</u> we can rely on.

_____

(5) Show me <u>that</u> you have in your pocket.

_____

(6) The package <u>what</u> arrived today was from my mother.

_____

(7) Our teacher, <u>that</u> usually comes on time, was late today.

_____

(8) She said she had not noticed him, <u>who</u> was a lie.

_____

3 日本語に合う英文になるように，空所に適切な語を入れましょう。

(1) 台所で料理をしているのが私の父です。

The man ＿＿＿＿＿＿＿ ＿＿＿＿＿＿＿ cooking in the kitchen is my father.

(2) 私は自分が好きな女の子の隣に座りました。

I sat next to the girl ＿＿＿＿＿＿＿ ＿＿＿＿＿＿＿ like.

(3) 向こうに見える木は樹齢700年を超えます。

The tree ＿＿＿＿＿＿＿ you ＿＿＿＿＿＿＿ see over there is over 700 years old.

(4) あなたが問題だと思うことを話してください。

Tell me ＿＿＿＿＿＿＿ ＿＿＿＿＿＿＿ ＿＿＿＿＿＿＿ is a problem.

(5) 私たちはその弁護士を雇ったのですが，彼も推薦したのでした。

We hired the lawyer, ＿＿＿＿＿＿＿ he also recommended.

(6) 彼はひとりでその人たちを助けようとしましたが，私はそれは難しいと思いました。

He tried to help them by himself, ＿＿＿＿＿＿＿ I found difficult.

4 日本語の意味に合うように，（　　　）内の語句を並べかえましょう。

(1) 英語が話せるスタッフはいますか。

Are there (who / English / staff members / can / any / speak)?

＿＿＿＿＿＿＿＿＿＿＿＿＿＿＿＿＿＿＿＿＿＿＿＿＿＿＿＿＿＿＿＿＿＿

(2) あなたが演奏している楽器は何といいますか。

What do you call (which / are / the instrument / playing / you)?

＿＿＿＿＿＿＿＿＿＿＿＿＿＿＿＿＿＿＿＿＿＿＿＿＿＿＿＿＿＿＿＿＿＿

(3) 私に与えられたお金をすべて使いました。

I spent (was / that / to me / all / given / the money).

＿＿＿＿＿＿＿＿＿＿＿＿＿＿＿＿＿＿＿＿＿＿＿＿＿＿＿＿＿＿＿＿＿＿

(4) 彼にそのプロジェクトを任せられる人がいますか。

Does he have anyone (can / to / leave / who / the project / he)?

＿＿＿＿＿＿＿＿＿＿＿＿＿＿＿＿＿＿＿＿＿＿＿＿＿＿＿＿＿＿＿＿＿＿

(5) 心配事をひとりで解決しようとしないでください。

Don't try to resolve (about / what / are / you / worried) by yourself.

＿＿＿＿＿＿＿＿＿＿＿＿＿＿＿＿＿＿＿＿＿＿＿＿＿＿＿＿＿＿＿＿＿＿

(6) 彼はしばしば約束を破る人です。

He is a person (breaks / his / who / promise / often).

＿＿＿＿＿＿＿＿＿＿＿＿＿＿＿＿＿＿＿＿＿＿＿＿＿＿＿＿＿＿＿＿＿＿

LESSON 11
関係詞① （関係代名詞）

教科書 pp.88-93

STEP 3 まとめ問題

1 （   ）内に与えられた語句を使い，英文を完成させましょう。

(1) 人間は火を使うことができる唯一の動物です。（ Human beings / that ）

_____

(2) 私たちは雇わなければならない人が 10 人必要です。（ whom ）

_____

(3) あなたが普段食べるものに気をつけてください。（ what ）

_____

2 日本語に合うように，英文を完成させましょう。

(1) 日本には世界的に有名な場所がたくさんあります。

Japan _____ worldwide.

(2) 私はあなたのためにできることをします。

I'll do _____

(3) ここが新しいスタジアムが建てられる場所です。

This is the place _____ at.

3 次の日本語を英語に直しましょう。

(1) これは使いやすいだけでなく，多くの情報が載っている本です。

_____

(2) あなたはスーツが似合いますね，めったに着ないけど。

_____

4 次の４つの項目を入れて，オリジナルの新製品を英語で発表しましょう。

① 製品名：Summer Fan Cooling Music Hat

② 冷却ファン（a cooling fan）とワイヤレスヘッドホンを備えた特殊な帽子

③ もちろん夏の暑さの中で頭部を冷やしておくために使えるものだが，お気に入りの音楽を聴きながらそれをすることができる

④ 値段：3,980 円

_____

_____

_____

_____

_____

_____

🔊 LISTENING

会話を聞いて，(1)～(4)の内容を書きとりましょう。

　拓とエイミーは，校外学習でペンの製造工程を見学しています。（*T*: Taku　*A*: Amy）

T:　Hey, Amy. Look at the conveyor belt! There are lots of pens on it.

A:　(1)_____! They look a little different from our usual pens.
　(2)_____.

T:　It says they are used not only for writing but also for emergencies. They are
　(3)_____!

A:　(4)_____ when we need to call for help? Aren't they great?

(1) _____

(2) _____

(3) _____

(4) _____

LESSON 12
関係詞② （関係副詞）

教科書 pp.96-101

STEP 1 基本問題

❶ 関係副詞 when / where

1　日本語の意味に合うように（　　）内の語句を並べかえ，文全体を書き直しましょう。

(1) あなたが言うことが理解できないときがあります。

There are (can't / I / times / understand / when) what you say.

_____

(2) 私は子どもの頃に住んでいた家を覚えています。

I remember (I / the house / where / lived) in my childhood.

_____

2　次の英文を日本語に訳しましょう。

(1) I will never forget the time when I first entered the classroom.

_____

(2) The stage is far from the seats where we are sitting.

_____

❷ 関係副詞 why

1　日本語の意味に合うように（　　）内の語句を並べかえ，文全体を書き直しましょう。

(1) 私が電話をしている理由は，あなたがそれに興味があるかどうかをたずねるためです。

(why / calling / I'm / the reason) is to ask you if you are interested in it.

_____

(2) 彼は口数が多すぎます。これが，彼女が彼を嫌う理由です。

He talks too much. (is / she / this / why) doesn't like him.

_____

2　次の英文を日本語に訳しましょう。

(1) The principal told the students the reason why school was canceled on Friday.

_____

(2) Please explain the reason why the event was canceled.

_____

❸ 関係副詞 how

1　日本語の意味に合うように（　　）内の語句を並べかえ，文全体を書き直しましょう。

(1) その本は彼がどのようにしてその島を発見したかについて語っています。

The book tells about (discovered / he / how) the island.

_____

(2) あなたの彼の扱い方はよくないと思います。

I think (the way / treat / you) him is not good.

_____

2　次の英文を日本語に訳しましょう。

(1) I was surprised at how she could get to such a far place.

_____

(2) This is how we made a decision about the festival.

_____

❹ 関係副詞の非制限用法

1　日本語の意味に合うように（　　）内の語を並べかえ，文全体を書き直しましょう。

(1) 私は 12 時まで彼を待って，それから昼食をとりました。

I waited for him until noon, (I / lunch / when / had).

_____

(2) 彼女は公園を歩いて通り，そこで数分間休憩しました。

She walked through the park, (rested / where / she) for a few minutes.

_____

2　次の英文を日本語に訳しましょう。

(1) In 1945, when World War II ended, my father was born.

_____

(2) He was hired as a cook at the restaurant, where he worked for five years.

_____

関係詞②（関係副詞）

STEP 2 実践問題

1 (）内から適切な語句を選びましょう。

(1) 2021 is the year (when / where) the Tokyo Olympics took place.

(2) He works at the company (which / where) I worked before.

(3) The reason (why / which) he quit his job is not clear.

(4) He took me to the office (where / which) we can get the ticket.

(5) Please show me (which / how) you drive the new car.

(6) It snowed on the day (how / when) I was born.

(7) That's the reason (why / how) I could arrive there in time.

(8) I can't believe (way / the way) he completed so much work.

(9) He didn't tell us (the time / the reason) why he was late.

(10) She stayed there until June, (which / when) she went back to America.

2 例にならって下線部の誤りを訂正し，文全体を書き直しましょう。

（例）My father always keep my promise. → My father always keeps his promise.

(1) Our school is at the site when a factory used to be.
_____

(2) Do you remember the days how we didn't even have money to buy rice?
_____

(3) I can't think of any reason which I don't go to school today.
_____

(4) Come to where the place we will meet.
_____

(5) This is which I escaped from danger.
_____

(6) This is the road when the accident happened.
_____

(7) I don't know the thing why she was successful.
_____

(8) I visited Fukuoka, why I happened to meet Taro.
_____

3 日本語に合う英文になるように，空所に適切な語を入れましょう。

(1) 火曜日はゴミを出す日です。

Tuesday is the ＿＿＿＿＿ ＿＿＿＿＿ we take out the garbage.

(2) 私は彼女が住んでいる街に引っ越しました。

I moved to the ＿＿＿＿＿ ＿＿＿＿＿ she lived.

(3) 彼がオフィスまで歩く理由は，彼は減量しなければならないからです。

The ＿＿＿＿＿ ＿＿＿＿＿ he walks to his office is because he must lose his weight.

(4) 6月は梅雨が始まる月です。

June is the ＿＿＿＿＿ ＿＿＿＿＿ the rainy season begins.

(5) 私たちは日本の農業がいかに守られるべきかを考える必要があります。

We have to think about ＿＿＿＿＿ Japanese agriculture should be protected.

(6) 彼は自分の経験を活かせる仕事に就きました。

He got a ＿＿＿＿＿ ＿＿＿＿＿ he could use his experience.

4 日本語の意味に合うように，（　　）内の語句を並べかえましょう。

(1) 私はそのイベントが行われる部屋を探しています。

I'm looking for (the event / the room / held / will / where / be).

＿＿＿＿＿＿＿＿＿＿＿＿＿＿＿＿＿＿＿＿＿＿＿＿＿＿＿

(2) 彼は私がその会社を辞めた日にその会社に入社しました。

He joined the company on (I / when / left / the day / the company).

＿＿＿＿＿＿＿＿＿＿＿＿＿＿＿＿＿＿＿＿＿＿＿＿＿＿＿

(3) 空気がきれいだということが私が田舎に住みたい理由です。

That the air is clean is (to / I / why / want / the reason / live) in the country.

＿＿＿＿＿＿＿＿＿＿＿＿＿＿＿＿＿＿＿＿＿＿＿＿＿＿＿

(4) 私がオフィスにいる午前中にオフィスに来てください。

Come to our office (when / there / on / I'm / the morning).

＿＿＿＿＿＿＿＿＿＿＿＿＿＿＿＿＿＿＿＿＿＿＿＿＿＿＿

(5) それがあなたが間違っている点です。

That's (the point / wrong / where / are / you).

＿＿＿＿＿＿＿＿＿＿＿＿＿＿＿＿＿＿＿＿＿＿＿＿＿＿＿

(6) こういうわけで私はあなたのアイディアに賛成しません。

(is / don't / this / I / agree / why) with your idea.

＿＿＿＿＿＿＿＿＿＿＿＿＿＿＿＿＿＿＿＿＿＿＿＿＿＿＿

LESSON 12
関係詞②（関係副詞）

教科書 pp.96-101

STEP 3 まとめ問題

1 （　　）内に与えられた語を使い，英文を完成させましょう。

(1) 私は私たちが桜を見るのを楽しむことができる春が好きです。(when)

_____

(2) あなたが出発する時間を教えてください。(time / when)

_____

(3) その歌手の歌い方は独特です。(how)

_____

2 日本語に合うように，英文を完成させましょう。

(1) 私は私たちが高校を卒業した日から彼に会っていません。

I haven't seen him _____

(2) 私たちがお互いを理解し合える日が来るでしょう。

_____ we can understand each other.

(3) このようにして彼女は自分の会社を大きくしました。

_____

3 次の日本語を英語に直しましょう。

(1) 私は彼がここにいない理由を知りません。

_____

(2) 私は午前中に出発しようとして，その時に電話が鳴りました。

_____

4 次の4つの項目を入れて，日本旅行を計画中の外国人にすすめる県を英語で説明しましょう。

① おいしい物を食べることができる場所に行きたいなら，宮城をすすめる

② 宮城は牛タンと呼ばれる牛の舌 (beef tongue) を食べることができる県である

③ 牛タンは一年中 (all the year round) 食べることができるが，夏に行くべき

④ 夏には仙台で美しい七夕祭り (the beautiful Tanabata Festival) を楽しめる

_____

_____

_____

_____

_____

🔊 LISTENING

会話を聞いて，(1)〜(4)の内容を書きとりましょう。

エイミーはロンに日本での観光について相談しています。(*A*: Amy　*R*: Ron)

A:　Do you know (1)_____ both beautiful nature and traditional Japanese buildings?

R:　You should visit Hida-furukawa. (2)_____ traditional Japanese culture.

A:　Sounds nice!

R:　What's more, the town was used as a setting for the famous movie *Your Name.*! (3)_____ for the first time!

A:　(4)_____ about *anime*.

(1) _____

(2) _____

(3) _____

(4) _____

仮定法
STEP 1 基本問題

❶ 仮定法過去

1　日本語の意味に合うように（　　）内の語句を並べかえ，文全体を書き直しましょう。

(1) 私があなたなら，彼と結婚するでしょう。

(were / I / if / you), I would marry him.

_____

(2) 彼はもっと一生懸命勉強すれば，試験に合格するのに。

(he / if / harder / studied), he would pass the exam.

_____

(3) 私たちはその列車に乗れば，そこに間に合って到着できるのに。

We could get there in time (the train / we / if / caught).

_____

2　次の英文を日本語に訳しましょう。

She would read this novel if she had enough time.

_____

_____

❷ 仮定法過去完了

1　日本語の意味に合うように（　　）内の語句を並べかえ，文全体を書き直しましょう。

(1) 昨日，天気が良かったら，私たちは出かけたのに。

(had / it / been / if) fine yesterday, we would have gone out.

_____

(2) 私がもし十分お金があったら，その車を買ったかもしれません。

(had / I / had / if) enough money, I might have bought the car.

_____

(3) もし彼の父親が彼を助けていたら，彼のビジネスはうまくいったのに。

If his father had helped him, (have / his business / gone / would) well.

_____

2　次の英文を日本語に訳しましょう。

If you had not followed the doctor's advice, you would have become sick.

_____

❸ wish を用いた仮定法

1 日本語の意味に合うように( )内の語を並べかえ，文全体を書き直しましょう。

(1) あなたがここにいればいいのに。

I (here / you / wish / were).

_____

(2) 彼が早く私に電話してくれたらよかったのに。

I (he / called / wish / had) me earlier.

_____

2 次の英文を日本語に訳しましょう。

I wish I had had more time to talk with you yesterday.

_____

❹ as if を用いた仮定法

1 日本語の意味に合うように( )内の語を並べかえ，文全体を書き直しましょう。

(1) 彼はまるで偉大な学者かのように話します。

He talks (if / were / as / he) a great scholar.

_____

(2) 彼は私をまるで以前に見たことがないかのように見ました。

He looked at me (had / as / he / if) not seen me before.

_____

2 次の英文を日本語に訳しましょう。

He cared for the girl as if she had been his child.

_____

LESSON 13

仮定法
STEP 2 実践問題

1 ( )内から適切な語句を選びましょう。

(1) If she (is / were) you, she would wait a little more.

(2) If you (can / could) live in Japan, where would you live?

(3) If you (came / had come) here yesterday, you could have heard the sound.

(4) If I (have known / had known) her address, I would have written to her.

(5) If she (uses / used) a PC well, she could find a job easily.

(6) If I had not contacted him, he (would not be / would have not been) here now.

(7) I wish I (am / were) still on holidays.

(8) He keeps the documents as if he (treats / treated) treasures.

(9) I wish you (continued / had continued) the job even now.

(10) She behaved as if nothing (happened / had happened).

2 例にならって下線部の誤りを訂正し，文全体を書き直しましょう。

（例）My father always keep my promise. → My father always keeps his promise.

(1) I will attend the meeting for you if I were asked.

_____

(2) If there had not been the information, we cannot have finished the project.

_____

(3) If it were not raining, we practice baseball.

_____

(4) If he saved money, he could have supported them then.

_____

(5) If I had not been busy at present, I would listen to you.

_____

(6) I feel as if I visit a foreign country.

_____

(7) I wish I could have hurry there right now.

_____

(8) He walked as if he was a model.

_____

78

3 日本語に合う英文になるように，空所に適切な語を入れましょう。

(1) もしお米がなければ，私は生きていけません。

I ＿＿＿＿＿＿＿＿ ＿＿＿＿＿＿＿＿ live if there was not rice.

(2) 天気がよかったなら，ピクニックは楽しかっただろうに。

If the weather ＿＿＿＿＿＿＿＿ ＿＿＿＿＿＿＿＿ fine, the picnic ＿＿＿＿＿＿＿＿ ＿＿＿＿＿＿＿＿ been enjoyable.

(3) 私があなたの立場なら，その申し出を受けるのに。

If I ＿＿＿＿＿＿＿＿ in your position, I ＿＿＿＿＿＿＿＿ accept the offer.

(4) あなたのサポートがあったならば，私たちはそれを時間内に終わらせられたのに。

We ＿＿＿＿＿＿＿＿ ＿＿＿＿＿＿＿＿ finished it in time ＿＿＿＿＿＿＿＿ your support.

(5) 彼に質問をしなかったらよかった。

I wish I ＿＿＿＿＿＿＿＿ ＿＿＿＿＿＿＿＿ asked him a question.

(6) 彼らはいつも，まるで周りに誰もいないかのように振舞います。

They always act as if ＿＿＿＿＿＿＿＿ ＿＿＿＿＿＿＿＿ no one around them.

4 日本語の意味に合うように，（　　）内の語を並べかえましょう。

(1) あなたがお腹がすいているのなら，喜んで何かつくるのに。

If you were hungry, I (to / be / make / would / something / happy) to eat.

＿＿＿＿＿＿＿＿＿＿＿＿＿＿＿＿＿＿＿＿＿＿＿＿＿＿＿＿＿＿＿＿＿＿

(2) もし彼が注意してなかったら，彼に何が起こっていただろうか。

If he had not been careful, (have / to / would / what / him / happened) ?

＿＿＿＿＿＿＿＿＿＿＿＿＿＿＿＿＿＿＿＿＿＿＿＿＿＿＿＿＿＿＿＿＿＿

(3) あなたが早く問題を報告すれば，解決するのがより簡単なのに。

If you reported a problem earlier, (would / it / to / easier / be / it / solve).

＿＿＿＿＿＿＿＿＿＿＿＿＿＿＿＿＿＿＿＿＿＿＿＿＿＿＿＿＿＿＿＿＿＿

(4) ここにいろと言われれば，私はどこにも行きませんでした。

If I (to / had / told / stay / been / here), I would not have gone anywhere.

＿＿＿＿＿＿＿＿＿＿＿＿＿＿＿＿＿＿＿＿＿＿＿＿＿＿＿＿＿＿＿＿＿＿

(5) 彼は数日間，寝ていないかのように見えます。

He looks (if / slept / had / as / he / not) for a few days.

＿＿＿＿＿＿＿＿＿＿＿＿＿＿＿＿＿＿＿＿＿＿＿＿＿＿＿＿＿＿＿＿＿＿

(6) 今日，仕事に行かなくていいのならいいのに。

(didn't / I / to / wish / have / I) go to work today.

＿＿＿＿＿＿＿＿＿＿＿＿＿＿＿＿＿＿＿＿＿＿＿＿＿＿＿＿＿＿＿＿＿＿

仮定法

STEP 3 まとめ問題

1 (　　　)内に与えられた語(句)を必要なら形を変えて使い，英文を完成させましょう。

(1) 彼らはお互い話し合えば，互いを理解するだろうに。(talk with / understand)

_____

(2) あなたが赤い色の方が好きだったのなら，私のものをあげたのに。(prefer / give)

_____

(3) 彼女はまるでネイティブスピーカーのように英語を話します。(as if / is)

_____

2 日本語に合うように，英文を完成させましょう。

(1) あなたが物事を説明するのが上手くなければ，だれかが代わりにするでしょう。

_____, someone would do it for you.

(2) もしあなたが運転免許を持っていなかったら，そこまでどうやって行ったでしょうか。

_____, how would you have been there?

(3) あらかじめ会議の準備をしておけばよかった。

_____ in advance.

3 次の日本語を英語に直しましょう。

(1) 車が欲しいのなら，インターネットで手頃な車を検索する方がいいだろう。

_____

(2) 彼女のアドバイスがなかったら，私たちは大きなミスをしただろう。

_____

APPLAUSE
ENGLISH LOGIC AND EXPRESSION I
Workbook

解答・解説

開隆堂

LESSON 1
現在と過去を表す表現

STEP 1　基本問題

❶1 (1) We're [We are] not busy on
　　 Saturdays.
　(2) The student runs very fast.
　(3) My brother usually goes to school
　　 by bus.
　(4) Lisa has some friends in London.
　2 (1) 私は私たちのバンドのリーダーを尊
　　 敬しています。
　(2) 彼女は高校で数学を教えています。

解説
❶1 (2)(3)(4) 現在を表す文で主語が三人称・単
　　 数になるので一般動詞に三単現の s を
　　 つける。

❷1 (1) His parents were at home.
　(2) We played tennis last Sunday.
　(3) I studied English yesterday.
　(4) We had a cute dog ten years ago.
　2 (1) 当時は［その頃は］たくさんの外国人
　　 が日本に来ました。
　(2) 私は高校生だった頃，この歌が好き
　　 でした。

解説
❷2 (1) in those days「当時は」

❸1 (1) We are [We're] doing our
　　 homework now.
　(2) He is [He's] taking a walk in the
　　 park now.
　(3) She is [She's] swimming in the
　　 pool now.
　(4) My brother is using my computer
　　 now.
　2 (1) 子どもたちは今，床に座っています。
　(2) 急ぎなさい。みんなが君を待ってい

ます。
❹1 (1) It was raining at nine yesterday.
　(2) They were talking about the plan
　　 then.
　(3) My mother was cooking in the
　　 kitchen when I got home.
　(4) Tom and his wife were enjoying
　　 their dinner.
　2 (1) その時，あなたは何を探していたの
　　 ですか。
　(2) 私は今朝7時にテレビを見ていまし
　　 た。

解説
❹2 (1) at that time「その時」

STEP 2　実践問題

1 (1) discovered　　(2) has
　(3) is watching　　(4) was reading
　(5) take　(6) put　(7) does
　(8) were　(9) had　(10) lay

解説
1 (9) 状態動詞はふつう進行形にしない。
　(10) 自動詞 lie の過去形 lay を選ぶ。lie on
　　 one's back「あおむけになる」

2 (1) One of my classmates is from Osaka.
　(2) The sun rises in the east.
　(3) I did not study hard when I was
　　 young.
　(4) We sat on the bank of the river and
　　 talked about our future.
　(5) Are the babies sleeping well now?
　(6) Where did your grandparents live in
　　 those days?
　(7) I was taking a bath when the
　　 doorbell rang.
　(8) Americans shake hands when they
　　 meet for the first time.

解説

2 (2)「東から」は，方角を表す in を用いて in the east で表す。

(8)「握手をする」は，常に複数形を用いて shake hands で表す。

3 (1) washes, after　(2) said, nothing

(3) are, lying　(4) were, running

(5) It, wasn't　(6) He's, reading

解説

3 (3) ie で終わる語は ie を y に変えて ～ ing をつける。lie → lying, die → dying

4 (1) often eats Chinese dishes

(2) taught her children French

(3) Are these students waiting

(4) Chris fell asleep while

(5) Hokkaido are you from

(6) What were you doing

解説

4 (2) 第 4 文型の文を作る。< teach ＋人＋もの>の順になる。

STEP 3　まとめ問題

1 (1) My grandfather is from England.

(2) (例 1) Our school had a large auditorium.

(例 2) There was a large auditorium in our school.

(3) They are lying on the beach now.

2 (1) (例 1) Her brother didn't eat anything (this morning.)

(例 2) Her brother ate nothing (this morning.)

(2) He usually lives in the country (, but at present) he is living in Tokyo.

(3) I fell asleep (while) I was studying.

解説

2 (3) while は「～している間」という意味の接続詞。

3 (1) The sun rises in the east.

(2) I was doing my homework at this time yesterday.

解説

3 (2)「昨日の今頃」は過去の一時点を表すので，過去進行形の文を使って表現する。

4 (例) My hero is Suda Masaki. He is an actor. He is appearing in a lot of movies and TV dramas. I became his fan three years ago. His performance is unique and impressive. (So I like him.)

LISTENING

(1) What are you reading

(2) As you know, his *manga* is very famous

(3) I respect him very much

(4) I became interested in Japanese culture

(5) You read that *manga* when you were a child

未来を表す表現

STEP 1　基本問題

❶ 1 (1) I think the temperature will rise next week.
　(2) "Ken is in hospital." "Oh, really? Then I'll visit him."
2 (1) あなた(方)はとても忙しそうなので，私は長居しません。
　(2) 大丈夫[心配しないで]。あなたのお気に入りのチームが試合に勝つでしょう。

解説
❶ 2 (1) will が主語の意志を表している。
　(2) 未来の出来事を予測している。

❷ 1 (1) Be careful. You are going to slip.
　(2) "Anne is in hospital." "Yes, I know. I'm going to visit her tomorrow."
2 (1) 彼女はとても疲れているようなので，寝てしまいそうです。
　(2) 彼はこの冬，長野でスキーをするつもりでいますが，彼の妻は彼の計画に反対しています。

解説
❷ 2 (1) 話し手の予測を表している。
　(2) 主語の予定を表している。

❸ 1 (1) Next Christmas falls on Sunday.
　(2) My plane arrives at Heathrow at noon tomorrow.
2 (1) あなたの乗る飛行機は明日，午前[朝の]5時に出ます[出発します]。
　(2) その映画は今夜何時に始まりますか。

解説
❸ 現在形は電車や飛行機の発着時間など，確定している未来のことを表すことができる。

❹ 1 (1) I'm visiting Barcelona this summer. I've already booked a hotel.
　(2) He is giving a farewell speech at the graduation ceremony tomorrow.
2 (1) 今夜はトムとディナーをとります[晩ごはんを食べることになっています]。
　(2) 急いで。あなたの乗る列車は2，3分で出てしまいます。

解説
❹ 進行形は，すでに決定していて準備をしている予定を表すことができる。

STEP 2　実践問題

1 (1) will be　　(2) It's going to
(3) leaves　　(4) visiting
(5) will　　(6) I'm going to
(7) I'm going to, I'm going to, I'll
(8) in　　(9) for

解説
1 (2) 「黒い雲を見て」と具体的な前兆があるため，be going to ～で表す。
(5) その場で決めた未来のことなので will を用いる。

2 (1) The weather forecast says it'll be [it will be] cloudy this weekend.
(2) My sister is going to be a doctor when she grows up.
(3) "Do you want to see a movie tomorrow?" "I'm playing [I'm going to play] tennis tomorrow."
(4) "I'm going out for lunch. And you?" "Sounds good, then I'll go with you."
(5) "Come downstairs. Dinner's ready." "I'm coming."

解説
2 (5) I'm coming. 「すぐ行きます」

3 (1) will, be　　(2) and, won't

　　(3) I'll, in　　(4) are, going

　　(5) We're, going　　(6) She's, meeting

解説

3 (2) ＜命令文，＋ and ～＞「…しなさい，そうすれば～」

　　(3) in ～「（現在を始点にして）～後に」

4 (1) leaves for London at noon

　　(2) The train for Osaka is leaving

　　(3) There will be a big earthquake in

　　(4) I'm going to be sick

　　(5) I will call you a doctor

　　(6) I'm going to quit soon

解説

4 (1) leave for ～「～に向けて出発する」

　　(5) call ～ a doctor「～に医者を呼ぶ」

STEP 3　まとめ問題

1 (1)（例1）Please tell me the truth. I won't [will not] tell anyone.

　　　（例2）Tell me the truth, please. I won't [will not] tell anyone.

　　(2) My brother is going to join the handball team when he enters high school.

　　(3) She's [She is] playing the piano at the graduation ceremony tomorrow.

解説

1 (3) 準備がすでに整っている予定のことなので現在進行形で表すとよい。

2 (1)（例1）He's [He is] going to lose the next match [game].

　　　（例2）We're [We are] going to lose the next game [match].

　　(2) it will rain [be rainy] the day after tomorrow.

　　(3)（例1）We're [We are] going to get married in

　　　（例2）We're [We are] getting married in

3 (1)（例1）The examination begins [starts] at nine o'clock tomorrow morning.

　　　（例2）The examination begins [starts] at 9 a.m. tomorrow.

　　(2) You look very busy.　I'll [I will] help you.

解説

3 (1) 確定している未来のことなので現在形で表す。

4 (例) I'm going to go to Yokohama with our foreign guest (s) on Saturday. It'll be cloudy and then fine on Saturday in Yokohama.　So we're going to visit Yokohama Chinatown. We're going to eat meat buns.　Then we're going to visit Yamashita Park and Aka Renga.

LISTENING

(1) can I ask you one thing

(2) a lot of Japanese have hay fever

(3) There is a lot of pollen on sunny and windy days

(4) it will be sunny tomorrow

(5) I guess they are going to wear masks

STEP 1 　基本問題

❶1(1) My sister can play the guitar very well, but I can't.
(2) "Can the news be true?" "It can't be."
(3) The boy could not be telling a lie.
2(1) 「スマホを借りてもいいですか」「すみません，駄目です」
(2) 「駅に行く道を教えていただけませんか」「ええ，いいですよ」

解説
❶1(2) 驚きを表す can の疑問文。
2(1) Can I ～? 「～してもいいですか」相手に許可を求める表現。
(2) Could you ～?「～していただけませんか」相手にていねいに依頼する表現。

❷1(1) Borrowers may take out three books at a time.
(2) You may or may not be wrong.
2(1) 「夕飯の前にデザートを食べてよいですか」「駄目に決まってるでしょう」
(2) ボブは今日欠席しています。病気かもしれません。

解説
❷2(2) might ～「～かもしれない」という推量を表す。might は may よりもやや可能性が低いことを表す。

❸1(1) Children must go home before dark.
(2) She must be tired after such a long walk.
(3) He should read the works of the novelist.

2(1) 私の日記を読んではいけません。
(2) あなたは自分の時間を無駄にすべきではありません。

解説
❸2(1) must not ～「～してはいけない」

❹1(1) Alice will be able to finish her homework by tomorrow.
(2) My brother has to get up at 5:30 a.m. on weekdays.
2(1) 私はその本を3時間で読むことができました。
(2) 彼は私を待つ必要はありません。

解説
❹2(2) don't[doesn't] have to ～「～する必要はない」

STEP 2 　実践問題

1 (1) couldn't 　　(2) should
(3) might 　(4) must 　(5) can't
(6) must 　(7) have to
(8) must not 　(9) was able to
(10) didn't have to

解説
1 (8) break *one's* promise「約束を破る」
(10) 文末に yesterday があるので，過去を表す didn't have to ～「～する必要はなかった」を選ぶ。

2 (1) I can read Chinese, but I cannot [can't] speak it.
(2) Don't believe him. He cannot [can't / could not] be telling the truth.
(3) She could read when she was four.
(4) His boss said that he might leave.
(5) Soon people will be able to go to the moon on holidays.
(6) Last week my son had an accident

and I had to take him to the hospital.

(7)（例 1）Should I take this medicine?

（例 2）Do I have to take this medicine?

(8) She does not [doesn't] have to follow his advice.

解説

2 (2) 可能性を表す can の否定形 can't [cannot]「～のはずがない」

(4) 時制の一致により，過去形の might にする。

(5) will be able to ～「～できるようになるでしょう」

3 (1) mustn't [can't], before [till / until]

(2) shouldn't, lies　　(3) don't, have

(4) Did, have　　　(5) I'll, be

(6) There, must

解説

3 (2) tell a lie [lies]「嘘をつく」

4 (1) Can you carry this baggage upstairs

(2) Should I wait and see for a while

(3) might catch cold in such light clothes

(4) You must not leave your garbage

(5) had to put up with the pain all night

(6) won't be able to return to your country

解説

4 (5) put up with ～「～を我慢する」

STEP 3　まとめ問題

1 (1)（例 1）"Can I take this book?" "No, you can't [cannot]."

（例 2）"May I take this book?" "No, you mustn't [must not]."

(2) "Must I [Do I have to] stay here?" "No, you don't [do not] have to."

(3) The team may [might / could] win the next game.

解説

1 (2) Must I ～? の疑問文に No で答えるときは，don't have to ～「～する必要はない」を用いて答える。

2 (1) Can [Will] you pass me the salt

(2) You can't [cannot] be hungry.

(3) Should I go to the dentist

解説

2 (1) Can [Will] you ～?「～してくれませんか」

3 (1) Your sister must be able to pass the entrance exam [examination].

(2) We'll [We will] have to leave home early tomorrow morning.

解説

3 (2) will have to ～「～しなければならないでしょう」

4 （例）When you climb Mt. Fuji, you don't have to bring so much food and water. You can buy food and water at the mountain huts. You can also use paid toilets there. But you must take your garbage home with you. (Please enjoy your climb!)

LISTENING

(1) This temple must be very famous

(2) this is my first visit to a Japanese temple

(3) you should take off your cap

(4) Can you tell me more about Japanese temples

LESSON 4 　　　　　　(pp.22-27)
完了形

STEP 1　基本問題

❶1(1) We have already had lunch.
　(2) Summer has passed.
　(3) Have you ever tried *natto*?
　(4) I have heard that song a few times.
　(5) They have lived in Kobe for two years.
　(6) I've been hungry since this morning.
　2(1) 彼は図書館に行ってしまいました(，ここにはいません)。
　(2) 彼はちょうどコンビニに行ってきたところです。
　(3) 彼は何回ハワイに行ったことがありますか。
　(4) 彼はどれくらい日本にいますか。

解説
❶2(1) have [has] gone to ～は「～へ行ってしまった(ここにいない)」。
　(2) have [has] been to ～は，完了用法では「～へ行ってきたところである」という意味。

❷1(1) It has been raining since this morning.
　(2) The children have been sleeping for at least ten hours.
　2 どれくらい日本語を勉強しているのですか。
❸1(1) We had just finished dinner when my father came home.
　(2) My grandfather had visited Paris many times before he died.
　(3) He had lived in Sydney for a couple of years before he moved to Kobe.
　2(1) 私たちがスタジアムに着いたとき，試合はすでに始まっていました。

　(2) 私はその女性に以前会ったことがあるのを覚えていました。
　(3) 初めて会ったとき，あなたはどのくらい教師をしていたのですか。

解説
❸1(1) just は had と過去分詞の間に置く。

STEP 2　実践問題

1(1) have been 　　(2) were
　(3) yet 　　(4) many times
　(5) long 　　(6) have known
　(7) been driving 　　(8) have lived
　(9) had lived 　　(10) when

解説
1(2) when 以降が過去を表しているので，主節は過去時制になる。
　(4) 回数を答えているので，How many times ～?「何回～」でたずねる。

2(1) Where did you see him last Saturday?
　(2) The student has been absent from school since yesterday.
　(3) It has been snowing since last night.
　(4) "Have you been to the hospital yet?" "No, I haven't."
　(5) I had had a headache for a week when I went to the doctor.
　(6) I had been watching television for three hours when my mother came home.
　(7) Where had your cat been before you found him?
　(8) Have you ever stayed at this hotel before?

解説
2(2) 現在完了が使われているため，起点を表す since yesterday「昨日から」にする。
　(4) 「～へ行ったところだ，～へ行ったこと

がある」は have been to 〜で表す。

(6) 過去の時点までの動作の継続を表すので
過去完了進行形になる。

3 (1) has, since   (2) had, before
(3) hasn't, yet   (4) It's, raining
(5) hadn't, fell   (6) She'd, for

解説
3 (2) 過去の時点までの経験を表しているので
過去完了形になる。
(5) fall asleep「眠りに落ちる」

4 (1) many times have they watched
(2) We've been pretty busy since
(3) have you been looking for
(4) had already gone to bed
(5) Had you ever spoken to
(6) had stayed in hospital for

解説
4 (3) 現在完了進行形の疑問文は< have [has]
＋主語＋ been 〜 ing ...? >。
(4) already は had と過去分詞の間に置く。

STEP 3　まとめ問題

1 (1) Have you been to the new shopping
mall yet?
(2) (例1) When we arrived at the station,
the train had already left.
(例2) The train had already left when
we arrived at the station.
(3) I've [I have] been doing my homework
for a couple of hours since I came
home.

解説
1 (1) have [has] been to 〜は，経験用法では
「〜へ行ったことがある」という意味。

2 (1) How many times have you been to
(2) How long has your sister been

looking for
(3) Where had you been before I visited
you

解説
2 (2) 「〜し続けている」と動作の継続を表し
ているので，現在完了進行形を用いる。

3 (1) She has lived in Osaka since she
moved to Japan.
(2) They had never seen snow before
they came to Japan.

解説
3 (2) 過去の時点までの経験を表しているので
過去完了形になる。never は had と過去
分詞の間に置く。

4 (例) I envy Kazu because he has been
abroad more than ten times. I have
never been abroad. I would like to
go to a foreign country, especially
Spain and watch a live soccer game
someday. In addition, I would like
to make friends with people there.

LISTENING

(1) How many times have you read that
manga
(2) I have read it at least ten times
(3) I have learned a lot of difficult *kanji*
(4) I'm not good enough yet

LESSON 5
受動態
(pp.28-33)

STEP 1　基本問題

❶1(1) English muffins are sold at that bakery.
　(2) The website is viewed by many people.
　(3) A lot of money was stolen from the safe.
2(1) あの国で英語は話されていますか。
　(2) あれらの絵は本当にバンクシーによって描かれたのですか。

解説
❶1 受動態の形は，＜ be 動詞＋過去分詞＞となり，行為者を表す場合は＜ by ＋行為者＞を直後に置く。

❷1(1) Three players were injured in the game.
　(2) My daughter is satisfied with the present.
2(1) 彼はその火事で亡くなりました。
　(2) 彼女はテストの結果にがっかりしていました。

解説
❷2(1) be killed は，「(事故, 災害, 戦争などで)死ぬ」という意味。

❸1(1) Mike was laughed at by his classmates today.
　(2) The dancing master is looked up to by his pupils.
2(1) 私は外国人に日本語で話しかけられました。
　(2) その選手[プレーヤー]はチームメイトに頼られています。

解説
❸1(1) laugh at ～「～を笑う」

(2) look up to ～「～を尊敬する」

❹1(1) The piano competition will be held in October next year.
　(2) Stars can't be seen in the daytime.
2(1) 今月は 21 日に満月が見られるかもしれません。
　(2) この教訓は忘れられるべきではない。

STEP 2　実践問題

1(1) is, visited, by　　(2) was, taken, to
　(3) were, made, in　　(4) are, sold, at
　(5) is, called, *tampopo*
　(6) was, satisfied, with
　(7) was, on, by　　(8) be, followed, by

解説
1(5) 5 文型の受動態では，補語を過去分詞の直後に置く。

2(1) I was taught French by my mother.
　(2) Spanish is not spoken in the country.
　(3) I was spoken to by an old woman in the park.
　(4) He was seriously injured in the traffic accident.
　(5) Are these chairs made of plastic?
　(6) Will the work be finished by tomorrow?

解説
2(2) 行為者ではなく，場所を表しているので in にする。
　(3) 群動詞 speak to ～「～に話しかける」の受動態にする。
　(5) イスの材料をたずねているので of にする。be made of ～「(材料)で作られる」

3(1) aren't, used　　(2) was, by
　(3) were, killed　　(4) I'm, disappointed
　(5) won't, be　　(6) be, to

10

解説

3 (2) 行為者の数をたずねる疑問文。by の目的語が How many people となり文頭に置かれた形。

4 (1) We are sent a Christmas card by
(2) called haggis and is commonly eaten
(3) Were those temples and shrines built
(4) Very few passengers were injured in
(5) may be laughed at by
(6) should not be included in

解説

4 (4) very few は「ほとんどない」という意味の準否定語。主語の passengers につき文全体が否定の意味になる。

STEP 3　まとめ問題

1 (1) (例 1) Comic books aren't sold at the bookstore.
(例 2) They don't sell comic books at the bookstore.
(2) Four people were injured in the traffic accident.
(3) The captain is looked up to by her [his] teammates.

解説

1 (2) be injured「怪我をする」

2 (1) (例 1) is cooked [prepared] by my father every weekend.
(例 2) is prepared [cooked] by my father on weekends.
(2) must be disappointed with [at] the result of the game.
(3) can't [cannot] be relied on [trusted].

解説

2 (2) 「～にちがいない」は must で表し，直後には原形の be を置く。

3 (1) (例 1) Canada has two official languages. English and French are spoken there.
(例 2) There are two official languages in Canada. English and French are spoken in the country.
(2) I was spoken to by a stranger this morning.

解説

3 (2) stranger「見知らぬ人」

4 (例) Let me introduce *okonomiyaki* to you. *Okonomiyaki* is a kind of Japanese pancake. It is made from flour, egg, cabbage, and so on. It is eaten by many people in Osaka and Hiroshima. It is very popular in Japan because it is cheap and delicious.

LISTENING

(1) I haven't seen this kind of bread before
(2) I bought its ingredients
(3) Here you are
(4) It is made from flour, butter

比較①（比較級，最上級）

STEP 1　基本問題

❶ 1 (1) This mobile phone is cheaper than that one.

(2) David can run faster than that athlete.

(3) Cricket is more popular than soccer in Sri Lanka.

2 彼女の夫は彼女よりゆっくりと英語を話します。

解説

❶ 2つのものや人を比べ，「〜よりも…」という意味を表すときには比較級を用いる。

❷ 1 (1) Australia is the smallest continent in the world.

(2) He gets up the earliest of all the members in the team.

(3) This is the most expensive item in this shop.

2 彼はその3人の男子の中でいちばん注意深く［丁寧に］その箱を運びました。

解説

❷ 3つ以上のものや人を比べ，「もっとも〜，いちばん〜」という意味を表すときには最上級を用いる。

❸ 1 (1) She is better at drawing pictures than her teacher.

(2) The economy of the country is worse than that of your country.

2 (1) 私の兄は家族の中でいちばん上手に料理をします。

(2) 彼はチームの全メンバーの中でいちばん下手に踊りました。

解説

❸ 1 (2) bad (悪い) — worse — worst

❹ 1 (1) She is a much better pianist than she was three years ago.

(2) The U.S.A has the third largest population in the world.

2 (1) 早く出発すればするほど，早くそこに着くことができます。

(2) ピカソは20世紀でもっとも偉大な芸術家の一人でした。

解説

❹ 1 (1) 比較級を強調する much「はるかに」は比較級の直前に置く。

(2) the ＋序数＋最上級「〜番目に…」

STEP 2　実践問題

1 (1) difficult　(2) worse　(3) younger　(4) earlier　(5) beautiful　(6) of　(7) of　(8) the most　(9) The more　(10) highest　(11) far

解説

1 (7) of the year「1年で」

(11) far は比較級を強調する語。

2 (1) My car is cheaper than yours.

(2) The tail of this dog is longer than that of my dog.

(3) (例1) It is much hotter today than yesterday.

(例2) It is far hotter today than yesterday.

(4) He looks more tired than he was last week.

(5) Is he the funniest of all your friends?

(6) (例1) The view from this building is the most beautiful in Tokyo.

(例2) The view from this building is the best in Tokyo.

(7) (例1) Nero was one of the worst emperors in Roman history.

(例2) Nero was the worst emperor in Roman history.

(8) The more he studied history, the more interested he became in it.

解説
2 (7)「もっとも～な…の1つ」は，＜one of the ＋最上級＋名詞の複数形＞で表す。

3 (1) larger, that　　(2) most, popular
(3) more, carefully　　(4) earlier, did
(5) the, best　　(6) The, older

解説
3 (6) the 比較級～, the 比較級…「～すればするほど，ますます…」

4 (1) became far more famous than
(2) much busier than they were
(3) better doctor than John does
(4) the question most quickly in
(5) is the third largest of
(6) one of the richest men

解説
4 (3) does は know のくり返しを避けるために用いられる代動詞。

STEP 3　まとめ問題

1 (1) He plays the piano better than his teacher.
(2) The higher you climb, the colder it becomes.
(3) This is one of the oldest temples in Kyoto.

2 (1) is the second largest of the six continents.
(2)(例1) drives most carefully [the most carefully] in her family.
(例2) is the most careful driver in her family.

(3)(例1) He is a much [far] better singer than he was
(例2) He is much [far] better at singing than he was
(例3) He sings much [far] better than he did

解説
2 (3) well(上手に)は不規則に変化する。well — better — best

3 (1) She is the youngest of the three sisters.
(2)(例1) Can [Will] you speak more slowly, please?
(例2) Could [Would] you speak more slowly (, please)?

解説
3 (2) 副詞 slowly「ゆっくりと」の比較級は more slowly。

4 (例) Let me talk about our challenge. The title is "The Biggest Daimonji." We, the Giant Slayers, are going to ask visitors to join us and form the biggest human letter 'dai' in the world. The Chinese character dai means 'big.' We are going to try to do this on the schoolyard during the school festival.

LISTENING

(1) It's bigger than our classroom
(2) What is it for
(3) the biggest poster in the world, aren't you
(4) it is one of the most interesting events

13

LESSON 7 (pp.40-45)
比較②（同等比較，倍数比較）

STEP 1　基本問題

❶ 1 (1) Our cat is as old as my sister.
(2) My husband plays golf as often as you do.
(3) Yesterday, it wasn't as hot as today.
2 私は母ほど朝早く起きることができません。

解説
❶ 2つのものや人を比べて「同じくらい〜」と表す場合，＜ as ＋形容詞・副詞＋ as 〜＞の形を使う。

❷ 1 (1) This bridge is twice as long as that one.
(2) The population of Tokyo is three times as large as that of your country.
2 (1) このスポーツカーはあなたの車の2倍の速さで走ることができます。
(2) 地球は月のおよそ4倍の大きさがあります。

解説
❷ 倍数表現は＜〜 times as ... as ＞で表す。2倍は〜 times の代わりに twice を用いる。

❸ 1 (1) My class has as many students as yours.
(2) I'll be back as soon as possible.
2 (1) 彼はあなたと同じ額のお金を持っています。
(2) 私の妻は相変わらず忙しいです。

解説
❸ 1 (2) as 〜 as possible「できるだけ〜」
2 (2) as 〜 as ever「相変わらず〜」

❹ 1 (1) Tokyo Skytree is taller than any other tower in the world.
(2) No other tower in the world is taller than Tokyo Skytree.
(3) No other lake in Japan is as large as Lake Biwa.
2 (1) 健康ほど大切なものはありません。
(2) かおるは私たちの学校のほかのどの生徒よりも早く登校します。

解説
❹ 1 (1) ＜比較級＋ than any other ＋名詞の単数形＞「ほかのどの〜よりも…」で最上級と同じ意味を表す。

STEP 2　実践問題

1 (1) smaller, than　(2) younger, than
(3) cooler, than　(4) doesn't, well
(5) less, than　(6) twice, hers
(7) three, times　(8) any, metal
(9) No, other　(10) Nothing, time

解説
1 (4) better は well「上手に」の比較級。
(6) half as 〜 as ... は「…の半分〜」

2 (1) My cousin has as many games as you have.
(2) (例1) My uncle drinks as much tea as an Englishman does.
(例2) My uncle drinks tea as often as an Englishman does.
(3) This milk is not as fresh as that (milk).
(4) (例1) Emma can run faster than any other boy in her class.
(例2) Emma can run faster than any boy in her class.

解説
2 (2) 「…と同じくらいの量の〜」は，＜ as much ＋名詞＋ as ＞で表す。

14

(3) 代名詞 one は不可算名詞を受けることは
できない。
(4) 肯定文で any が使われるとき，後ろの名
詞は単数形となる。

3 (1) as, carefully　　(2) isn't, as
(3) twice, mine　　(4) It, ever
(5) soon, possible　　(6) No, other

解説
3 (3) 「私の部屋」は所有代名詞 mine（= my
room）を用いる。
(6) no(other) + 名詞 + 動詞 + as 原級 as 〜
「〜ほど…な名詞はない」

4 (1) cheap as that old one
(2) the piano as well as
(3) five times as many books
(4) as much information as possible
(5) mathematics as hard as ever
(6) more popular than any other

解説
4 (3) 数が同等であることを表すときは，< as
many + 名詞の複数形 + as >で表す。

STEP 3　まとめ問題

1 (1) My digital camera is not as expensive
as this one.
(2) The population of Mexico is almost
as large as that of Japan.
(3) I will reply as soon as possible.

解説
1 (2) that は population のくり返しを避ける
ために用いられる代名詞。

2 (1) is about ten times as large as Japan.
(2) has twice as many students as yours.
(3) (例 1) No other tower in the world
was as tall as
(例 2) No other tower in the world
was taller than

解説
2 (3) 「エッフェル塔ほど（より）高い塔はな
かった」と考える。

3 (1) She walked as slowly as my
grandmother.
(2) I want to read as many books as
possible during the summer vacation.

解説
3 (2) 「できるだけたくさんの本」は as many
books as となる。many は数量形容詞な
ので直後に名詞の複数形を置くことに注
意する。直後に不可算名詞を置く場合は
much を用いる。

4 (例) People in Japan are wasting twice
as much food as people in the world
need. We throw a lot of food away
because we leave it unfinished.
This is a very serious problem, so
we should do something about it. I
think we should stop buying more
food than we need.

LISTENING

(1) I have never seen a lunch like this
(2) is much healthier than fast food
(3) I like cooking as much as watching
anime
(4) I'll teach you how to make a Japanese
bento

LESSON 8 　　　　　(pp.46-51)
動名詞，to 不定詞①（名詞的用法）

STEP 1　基本問題

❶ 1 (1) Getting up early is easy for me.
　 (2) His favorite pastime is cooking.
　 (3) We finished cleaning our classroom.
　 2 あなたはいつ英語の勉強を始めました
　　 か。

解説

❶ 1 (3) finish は目的語に動名詞をとり，「～し
　　　 終える」。
　 2 begin は目的語に動名詞および不定詞をと
　　 り，「～し始める」。

❷ 1 (1) Takuya is good at playing the
　　　 guitar.
　 (2) We look forward to hearing from
　　　 you.
　 (3) I am used to living in the country.
　 2 エイミーは友だちをつくるのが得意で
　　 すか。

解説

❷ 1 (2) look forward to ～ing で「～すること
　　　 が楽しみである」。to は前置詞。
　 (3) be used to ～ing で「～することに慣
　　　 れている」。to は前置詞。

❸ 1 (1) To exercise every day is difficult for
　　　 me.
　 (2) His hobby is to make cakes.
　 (3) I want to visit Canada.
　 (4) My mother told me to carry the
　　　 chair.
　 2 彼に沢田さんに電話するよう頼んでく
　　 ださい。

解説

❸ 1 (4) tell + O + to ～で「O に～するように
　　　 言う」。

2 ask + O + to ～で「O に～するように頼
　 む」。

❹ 1 (1) It is easy for them to remember the
　　　 rule.
　 (2) It is kind of him to drive me there.
　 (3) We found it difficult to start a new
　　　 job.
　 2 私たちがその川で泳ぐのは危険ですか。

解説

❹ 1 (3) < find it ～ to ... >「…するのは～だ
　　　 とわかる」。it は形式目的語で，to ～以
　　　 下を表す。

STEP 2　実践問題

1 (1) Watching　　(2) having
　 (3) making　　(4) joining
　 (5) playing　　(6) to eat
　 (7) to study　　(8) to show
　 (9) for him, to get　　(10) to finish

解説

1 (7) decide to ～「～することに決める」
　 (8) want + 人 + to ～「人に～してもらいた
　　　 い」

2 (1) Her dream is to work [working] for
　　　 world peace.
　 (2) I like running [to run] in the park
　　　 before breakfast.
　 (3) The driver practiced parking her car.
　 (4) She is good at teaching math.
　 (5) Thank you for inviting me.
　 (6) Kei hopes to get a new mobile phone.
　 (7) It is important for us to get enough
　　　 rest.
　 (8) I found it interesting to listen to the
　　　 expert's opinions.

解説

2 (3) practice ～ing「～することを練習する」

(5) for は前置詞なので，後ろに動名詞を置く。

(6) hope to ～「～したいと望む」

3 (1) Using　(2) stopped, raining
(3) to, speaking　(4) sending
(5) to, make　(6) of, to

解説

3 (4) forget ～ ing「～したことを忘れる」

(6) It is ... of 人 + to ～「～するなんて，人が…だ」…が人の性質を表す語のときは of となる。

4 (1) Did you enjoy staying in
(2) Remember to do your homework
(3) Are you interested in learning
(4) do you want to be
(5) Was it easy for you to
(6) found it hard to choose

解説

4 (2) remember to ～「～することを覚えている，忘れずに～する」

(3) in は前置詞なので，後ろに動名詞を置く。

STEP 3　まとめ問題

1 (1) I cannot finish writing many letters.
(2) He wants to be good at singing English songs.
(3) She often forgets to take her smartphone.

解説

1 (3) forget to ～「～することを忘れる（し忘れる）」

2 (1) My dream is to visit [visiting] some temples
(2) My mother told me to give the flowers
(3) It is important for us to prepare

解説

2 (2) tell + 人 + to ～「人に～するように言う」

3 (1) All of us tried to help the cat.
(2) Many people found it necessary to know how to get to the shelter.

解説

3 (1) try to ～「～しようとする」

4 (例) There are two things to do before a typhoon is forecast. First, it is necessary to get a disaster prevention map and know how to get to the shelter. Second, it is important to prepare an emergency bag and check the items you put in it. Providing is preventing, you know.

LISTENING

(1) in the shelter with cardboard
(2) I'd like to learn various uses of cardboard
(3) How about joining the disaster drill
(4) I'd love to

17

LESSON 9 (pp.52-57)
to 不定詞②（形容詞的用法，副詞的用法）

STEP 1　基本問題

❶1 (1) I want something hot to drink.
　　(2) He had no friend to help him.
　2 彼女は私たちに見せる(ための)写真を
　　たくさん持っています。

解説
❶1 (1) something hot to drink「飲むための
　　温かいもの」→「温かい飲み物」

❷1 (1) We went to the park to play tennis.
　　(2) Our father lived to be 80 years old.
　　(3) I'm happy to hear the news.
　2 (1) 彼は辞書を買うために本屋に行きま
　　した。
　　(2) 彼女は成長して有名な作家になりま
　　した。
　　(3) 私はまたあなたにお目にかかれてう
　　れしいです。

解説
❷1 (2) live to be ～「～歳まで生きる」
　　(3) be happy to ～「～してうれしい」
　2 (2) grow up to be ～「成長して～になる」

❸1 (1) My doctor told me not to eat too
　　much.
　　(2) It is important not to talk with
　　your classmates during class.
　2 私の母は私たちに夜更かししないよう
　　に言いました。
❹1 (1) My brother is too young to take
　　that job.
　　(2) She is rich enough to have a few
　　cars.
　　(3) We left early in order to be in time.
　　(4) Could you tell me how to get to the
　　station?

2 昨日は暑すぎて，外出できませんでし
　た。

解説
❹1 (1) too ～ to ...「～すぎて…できない」「…
　　するには～すぎる」
　　(2) ～ enough to ...「…するほど(十分)～
　　である」「十分…なので，…できる」
　　(4) how to ～「～のしかた，～する方法」

STEP 2　実践問題

1 (1) to visit　　(2) to do
　(3) to borrow　　(4) to see
　(5) not to come　　(6) to go
　(7) too busy to take　　(8) old enough to
　(9) in order to avoid　　(10) what to do

解説
1 (4) be surprised to ～「～して驚いている」
　(5) 不定詞の否定形は not を to の前に置く。
　(9) in order to ～「～するために」
　(10) what to do「何をすべきか」

2 (1) She left work early to see a dentist.
　(2) I had no time to have lunch today.
　(3) Would you ask him not to bother us?
　(4) What did he come to Japan to do?
　(5) Is it better for us not to climb a
　　mountain during winter?
　(6) We took a taxi in order not to miss
　　the train.
　(7) He is clever enough not to repeat the
　　same mistake.
　(8) Please tell me when to leave.

解説
2 (4) to do は目的を表す「(何を)するために」
　(8) when to ～「いつ～すればいいのか」

3 (1) to, write　　(2) not, to
　(3) in, order, to　　(4) too, to

18

(5) enough, to   (6) where, to, to

解説

3 (2) be sorry to (not to) ～「～して(～しなくて)すまないと思う，気の毒に思う」

4 (1) things she wants to try
   (2) went to the airport to see
   (3) for you not to do anything
   (4) played well only to lose the game
   (5) too hot for me to drink
   (6) which route to take to arrive

解説

4 (4) only to ～「その結果，～しただけである」望ましくない結果を表す。
   (6) which ～ to ...「どの～を…すればいいのか」

STEP 3　まとめ問題

1 (1) I study English to travel abroad.
   (2) The movie is good enough to watch again.
   (3) Ken was too tired to make dinner.

2 (1) I went to the store to buy / to scare away
   (2) He was surprised to read
   (3) for her not to tell

解説

2 (1) to buy は目的を表す不定詞で，to scare away は a tool を修飾する形容詞的用法の不定詞。

3 (1) She stopped to talk with [to] me.
   (2) I want to learn how to make wine.

解説

3 (1) stop to ～「～するために立ち止まる」
   stop ～ ing は「～することをやめる」

4 (例) This square cloth is called *furoshiki*. It is a traditional tool to wrap and carry things. You can use it to wrap your *bento* lunch box in your daily life. You can also use it for an eco-friendly bag when you buy something. It is useful even in case of an emergency. (I hope you will like it.)

LISTENING

(1) What's the matter
(2) for me to scare it away
(3) come to think of it
(4) It's about a tool to scare away flies

STEP 1 基本問題

❶ 1 (1) Her sleeping baby looks happy.
　(2) Can you open the closed windows in the house?
　2 (1) 私たちは彼女の興味深いスピーチを聴くことができました。
　(2) 誰がその壊れたいすを直したのですか。

【解説】

❶ 現在分詞(sleeping, interesting)や過去分詞(closed, broken)1語で名詞を修飾する場合，分詞は名詞の前に置く。

❷ 1 (1) The boy swimming over there is Takeshi.
　(2) This is a building built by our company.
　2 (1) 私は私の隣に座っている男性に話しかけました。
　(2) その国では何語が話されていますか。
　(3) これはイタリアで作られたシャツです。

【解説】

❷ 分詞を含んだ複数の語句(swimming over there, built by our company)で名詞を修飾する場合，名詞の後に置く。

❸ 1 (1) He remained standing for two hours.
　(2) I kept the door locked.
　2 (1) その事実は多くの人に知られていないままであった。
　(2) 水を出しっぱなしにしないでください。

【解説】

❸ 1 (1) ＜ remain + 現在分詞(過去分詞)＞は

「～したままである(～されたままである)」。
　(2) ＜ keep + O + 現在分詞(過去分詞)＞は「O を～している(～された)状態にしておく」。
　2 (2) ＜ leave + O + 現在分詞(過去分詞)＞は「O を～している(された)ままにしておく」。

❹ 1 (1) I saw him calling someone.
　(2) We heard her laughing in the next room.
　(3) My mother felt the building shaking.
　2 (1) あなたは彼らがその部屋に入っていくのを見ましたか。
　(2) 私は彼女がフランス語を話しているのを聞いたことがあります。

【解説】

❹ 1 ＜知覚動詞 + O + 現在分詞＞「O が～しているのを…する」の語順で並べる。

STEP 2 実践問題

1 (1) excited　(2) boring
　(3) made　(4) surrounding
　(5) visiting　(6) taken
　(7) waiting　(8) damaging
　(9) destroyed　(10) apologizing

【解説】

1 (1) excited「(人が)興奮した」exciting「(物事が人を)興奮させる」
　(2) boring「退屈させる」bored「(人が)退屈している」
　(8) damaging「被害を与える」damaged「被害を受ける」

2 (1) It is a surprising fact.
　(2) All of us removed the fallen leaves.
　(3) No one lives in the burning [burned] house.

(4) We know the girl wearing glasses.

(5) This is a machine designed to work faster.

(6) She showed a satisfied look.

(7) You must keep the machine running.

(8) I heard my name called by someone.

解説

2 (1) surprised「驚いた」surprising「驚くべき」

(6) satisfying「満足させる」satisfied「満足した」show a satisfied look で「満足そうな顔を見せる」という意味。

3 (1) written, in   (2) happening, there

(3) reserved, by   (4) kept, doing

(5) felt, tired   (6) her, calling

解説

3 (4) keep 〜 ing「〜し続ける」

(5) tired「疲れた」tiring「疲れさせる」

4 (1) don't know the woman waving her hand

(2) sell calendars printed by the company

(3) rope connecting the two cars is

(4) the bus painted with pictures of animals

(5) found a small box placed at the corner

(6) watched him leaving his house early

解説

4 (5) < find + O + 現在分詞（過去分詞）>「O が〜している（〜される）のを見つける」

STEP 3　まとめ問題

1 (1) I received an email offering me a job.

(2) It is something [the thing] stolen from my house.

(3) She became interested in working for the company.

解説

1 (3) interested「興味を持っている」
interesting「興味を引き起こす」

2 (1) developing many kinds of smartphones

(2) The man injured in the accident

(3) She kept [left] them waiting

解説

2 (2) injured「負傷した」injuring「負傷させる」

3 (1) She gave us a letter encouraging us.

(2) The situation remained unchanged for a long time.

解説

3 (1) encouraging「勇気づける」encouraged「勇気づけられる」

4 （例）

A: Do you see the boys playing baseball?

B: Yes, I do.

A: I see one of them having a broken bat. Perhaps he is apologizing to the other boys. Do you know him?

B: Do you mean the boy wearing a red cap?

A: Yes.

B: He is one of my classmates, Shohei.

LISTENING

(1) Your smiling face tells me everything

(2) I saw you with a cute girl wearing a cap

(3) she showed us her cap designed by a famous artist

(4) She looked quite different

LESSON 11
関係詞①（関係代名詞）

(pp.64-69)

STEP 1　基本問題

❶1(1) She has a friend who lives in Australia.
　(2) The month which comes after March is April.
　(3) I read a letter that was written in English.
　2 きれいな庭がある家が見えますか。

解説

❶ 主格（主語の働きをする）の関係代名詞は先行詞（修飾される語句）が人の場合は who や that，ものの場合は which や that を用いる。

❷1(1) The man whom she married is a nurse.
　(2) This is the chair which I bought yesterday.
　(3) The movie that I saw yesterday was boring.
　2 あなたがパーティーで会った女性は私の姉[妹]です。

解説

❷ 目的格（目的語の働きをする）の関係代名詞は先行詞が人の場合は whom（who）や that，ものの場合は which や that を用いる。

❸1(1) What we need is the data.
　(2) That is what you said yesterday.
　(3) I believe what he told me.
　2(1) 彼は以前の彼ではありません。
　(2) 私はあなたに望むものを送ります。

解説

❸ 関係代名詞 what が導く節は名詞節で，「～するもの，こと」を表し，主語や目的語の働きをする。

❹1(1) I have a brother, who works as a writer.
　(2) She lent me the DVD, which was not interesting.
　2(1) 彼女には息子が2人いて，2人は同じ高校に通っている。
　(2) 彼は高価なスーツを持っていて，それはイタリア製です。

解説

❹1(1) 関係代名詞の非制限用法は先行詞（a brother）について補足的に説明する。

STEP 2　実践問題

1(1) which　　(2) who　　(3) that
　(4) whom　　(5) which　　(6) that
　(7) what　　(8) which　　(9) whom
　(10) which

解説

1(10) 非制限用法の which はその前の文の一部または全部を先行詞とすることができる。

2(1) English is a language which [that] is spoken in many countries.
　(2) The people who [that] live here are very kind.
　(3) This is the pen which [that] the author wrote the novel with.
　(4) He's the person whom [who] we can rely on.
　(5) Show me what you have in your pocket.
　(6) The package which [that] arrived today was from my mother.
　(7) Our teacher, who usually comes on time, was late today.
　(8) She said she had not noticed him, which was a lie.

2 (7) 関係代名詞の that は通常，非制限用法
としては使わない。

(8) she had not noticed him が先行詞となる
非制限用法の文なので which を使う。

---

3 (1) who, is　　(2) whom [that], I

(3) which [that], can

(4) what, you, think　　(5) whom

(6) which

---

3 (4) what you think is a problem は what
is a problem「問題であること」に you
think を挿入した形。

(6) which は to help them by himself「ひと
りでその人たちを助けること」が先行詞。

---

4 (1) any staff members who can speak
English

(2) the instrument which you are playing

(3) all the money that was given to me

(4) who he can leave the project to

(5) what you are worried about

(6) who often breaks his promise

---

4 (5) resolve の目的語となる名詞節を作る。
what は，節内では about の目的語。

STEP 3　まとめ問題

1 (1) Human beings are the only animals
that can use fire.

(2) We need ten people whom we must
employ.

(3) Be careful about what you usually
eat.

2 (1) has many places which [that] are
famous

(2) what I can do for you.

(3) which a new stadium will be built

---

2 (3) at the place「その場所に」の the place
が先行詞として前に出ているので，最後
の at は必要。

---

3 (1) This is a book that is not only easy to
use but also has much information.

(2) You look good in a suit, which you
rarely wear.

---

3 (1) not only A but also B「A だけでなく B も」

---

4 （例）We'd like to show you our new
product, Summer Fan Cooling
Music Hat! It's a special hat which
has a cooling fan and wireless
headphones. Of course, this is
what you can use to keep your head
cool in the summer heat, but you
can do it while you are listening
to your favorite music. The price
is only 3,980 yen. (You should buy
one! Thank you.)

LISTENING

(1) That's amazing

(2) Tell me what the guidebook says

(3) pens which have a light and a whistle

(4) Do you mean we can use them

関係詞②（関係副詞）

STEP 1　基本問題

❶1(1) There are times when I can't understand what you say.

(2) I remember the house where I lived in my childhood.

2(1) 私は初めてその教室に入った時のことを決して忘れません。

(2) ステージは私たちが座っている席から遠いです。

解説
❶ when は時間，where は場所を先行詞として説明する時に使う。

❷1(1) The reason why I'm calling is to ask you if you are interested in it.

(2) He talks too much. This is why she doesn't like him.

2(1) 校長は生徒たちに，金曜日に学校が休校になった理由を話しました。

(2) そのイベントが中止になった理由を説明してください。

解説
❷1(2) This is why ～ .「こういうわけで～，これが～である理由だ」

2(1)(2) the reason why ～「～する理由」

❸1(1) The book tells about how he discovered the island.

(2) I think the way you treat him is not good.

2(1) 私はどうやって彼女がそんなに遠い所に到着できたかに驚きました。

(2) このようにして私たちはお祭りについての決定をしました。

解説
❸2(2) This is how ～「このようにして～」

❹1(1) I waited for him until noon, when I had lunch.

(2) She walked through the park, where she rested for a few minutes.

2(1) 1945 年は第二次世界大戦が終わった年ですが，その年に私の父は生まれました。

(2) 彼はそのレストランでコックとして雇われ，そこで彼は 5 年間働きました。

解説
❹ 非制限用法の when や where は時間や場所について補足的に説明する時に使う。

1(1) ここでは非制限用法の when が「それから(and then)」という意味を表している。

STEP 2　実践問題

1 (1) when　　(2) where　　(3) why
(4) where　　(5) how　　(6) when
(7) why　　(8) the way　　(9) the reason
(10) when

解説
1 (5) how は方法(どのようにするか)を表すときに使う関係副詞で，the way で置きかえることができる。

2 (1) Our school is at the site where a factory used to be.

(2) Do you remember the days when we didn't even have money to buy rice?

(3) I can't think of any reason why I don't go to school today.

(4) Come to the place where we will meet.

(5) This is how I escaped from danger.

(6) This is the road where the accident happened.

(7) I don't know the reason why she was successful.

(8) I visited Fukuoka, where I happened to meet Taro.

解説
2 (1) at the site「その場所に」

3 (1) day, when　　(2) town [city], where
(3) reason, why　　(4) month, when
(5) how　　(6) job, where

解説
3 (6) where の先行詞が「場合，立場，状況」を表す語のときもある。

4 (1) the room where the event will be held
(2) the day when I left the company
(3) the reason why I want to live
(4) on the morning when I'm there
(5) the point where you are wrong
(6) This is why I don't agree

解説
4 (5) 関係副詞 where は point「点」を先行詞として使われることもある。

STEP 3　まとめ問題

1 (1) I like spring when we can enjoy seeing cherry blossoms.
(2) Please tell me the time when you leave.
(3) How the singer sings is unique.
2 (1)（例 1）since the day when we graduated from high school.
（例 2）since we graduated from high school.
(2) The day will come when
(3) This is how she made her company bigger.

解説
2 (2) The day (the time) will come when ～
「～する日 (時) が来るでしょう」

3 (1) I don't know the reason why he is not here.
(2) I was about to leave in the morning, when the phone rang.
4 (例) If you want to visit a place where you can eat delicious food, I'll recommend Miyagi. It's a prefecture where you can eat beef tongue called *gyutan*. You can eat *gyutan* all year round, but you should go there in summer, when you can enjoy the beautiful Tanabata Festival in Sendai.

LISTENING

(1) a sightseeing spot where we can enjoy
(2) That is a place where you can explore
(3) I'll never forget the day when I watched it
(4) You look really excited when you talk

LESSON 13 (pp.76-81)
仮定法

STEP 1　基本問題

❶1 (1) If I were you, I would marry him.
　(2) If he studied harder, he would pass the exam.
　(3) We could get there in time if we caught the train.
2 彼女に十分な時間があれば，この小説を読むのに。

解説
❶1 (1) 仮定法過去の if 節では，be 動詞は were を使う。

❷1 (1) If it had been fine yesterday, we would have gone out.
　(2) If I had had enough money, I might have bought the car.
　(3) If his father had helped him, his business would have gone well.
2 あなたが医師の助言に従わなかったら，病気になったでしょう。

解説
❷1 仮定法過去完了の主節は，＜助動詞の過去形＋ have ＋過去分詞＞の形になる。

❸1 (1) I wish you were here.
　(2) I wish he had called me earlier.
2 昨日，あなたと話す時間がもっとあったらよかったのに。
❹1 (1) He talks as if he were a great scholar.
　(2) He looked at me as if he had not seen me before.
2 彼はその女の子をまるでわが子のように世話をしました。

解説
❸❹I wish や as if の後は現在のことであれ

ば過去形(be 動詞は were)，過去のことであれば，過去完了形となる。

STEP 2　実践問題

1 (1) were　　(2) could
　(3) had come　　(4) had known
　(5) used　　(6) would not be
　(7) were　　(8) treated
　(9) continued　　(10) had happened

解説
1 (6)「私が彼に連絡しなかったら，彼は今，ここにいないだろう。」if 節で過去に関することを仮定し(仮定法過去完了)，主節では現在のことへの想像を述べている(仮定法過去)。

2 (1) I would attend the meeting for you if I were asked.
　(2) If there had not been the information, we could not [couldn't] have finished the project.
　(3) If it were not raining, we would [could] practice baseball.
　(4) If he had saved money, he could have supported them then.
　(5) If I were not [weren't] busy at present, I would listen to you.
　(6) I feel as if I visited a foreign country.
　(7) I wish I could hurry there right now.
　(8) He walked as if he had been a model.

解説
2 (5) at present は「現在」という意味なので，仮定法過去の形となる。

3 (1) could, not
　(2) had, been, would, have
　(3) were, would
　(4) could, have, with
　(5) had, not [never]

(6) there, were

解説

3 (4) with ～「～があれば」with your support
= if we had had your support

4 (1) would be happy to make something
(2) what would have happened to him
(3) it would be easier to solve it
(4) I had been told to stay here
(5) as if he had not slept
(6) I wish I didn't have to

解説

4 (5) as if 以下は，数日前から現在まで続くこ
とを表現しているので，過去完了形とな
る。

STEP 3　まとめ問題

1 (1) If they talked with each other, they
would understand each other.
(2) If you had preferred the red one, I
would have given you mine.
(3) She speaks English as if she were a
native speaker.

解説

1 (2) prefer「より好む」の過去分詞は，r を
重ねて preferred となる。

2 (1) If you were not good at explaining
things
(2) If you had not had a driver's license
(3) I wish I had prepared for the
meeting

3 (1) If you wanted a car, it would be
better to search for a reasonable one
on the Internet.
(2) Without her advice, we would have
made a big mistake.

解説

3 (2) without ～「～がなかったら（なければ）」
without her advice ＝ If we had not
gotten her advice

4 （例）I regret that I scored on my own
team during the last soccer game.
When I asked Kazu to give me
advice, he said, "If I were you, I
would never forget about it in order
to practice harder.　But if I were
you, I wouldn't worry too much
because I know you are a far better
defender than you were six months
ago."　If I hadn't got advice from
him, I would have given up.　I'll do
my best to be the best defender in
the team.

LISTENING

(1) you are searching for something on the
Internet
(2) I wish supermarkets in Japan had meat
pies
(3) If I were good at cooking, I could make
them
(4) I'll help you make them

STEP 1　基本問題

❶1(1)(例1) When she was eleven years old, her family moved to Osaka.

(例2) Her family moved to Osaka when she was eleven years old.

(2)(例1) Before her husband had supper, he had taken a bath.

(例2) Her husband had taken [took] a bath before he had supper.

(3)(例1) After I finish my homework, I will play the video game.

(例2) I will play the video game after I finish my homework.

2(1) 雨が止むまでここで暇をつぶしましょう。

(2) 彼は警官を見たとたんに逃げ去りました。

解説

❶1(3) 時と条件を表す副詞節の中では，未来のことでも現在形で表す。

❷1(1)(例1) Because my brother was ill, he was absent from school.

(例2) My brother was absent from school because he was ill.

(2)(例1) As our captain is a hardworking person, we respect her.

(例2) We respect our captain as she is a hardworking person.

2 君は高熱があるのだから，今日は外出すべきではありません。

❸1(1)(例1) If it rains tomorrow, I will stay at home.

(例2) I will stay at home if it rains tomorrow.

(2)(例1) Though my father was very tired, he went on working.

(例2) My father went on working though he was very tired.

2(1) たとえ高価であっても，あなたはそれを購入すべきです。

(2) 緊急でなければ，あなたはこのボタンを押してはいけません。

❹1(1) He spoke so fast that I couldn't understand him.

(2) It was such a good movie that I saw it twice.

(3) Let's leave now so that we can catch the train.

2(1) このところ[最近]彼女はとても忙しいので，読書する時間がありません。

(2) ネコが出て行けるように，ドアを開けてください。

STEP 2　実践問題

1 (1) that 　　(2) As soon as

(3) until 　　(4) before

(5) since 　　(6) because 　　(7) Since

(8) if 　　(9) unless 　　(10) Though

(11) so 　　(12) such 　　(13) so that

解説

1 (3) until「〜までずっと」は継続を表す接続詞。

2 (1) He got up before the sun rose.

(2) I will come back before it gets dark.

(3) If my father cooks dinner, I will help him.

(4) I'll buy it if it is not very expensive.

(5) Though he is not very tall, he is a good basketball player.

(6) I was so excited that I could not sleep last night.

(7) It rained so heavily that they gave up playing golf.

3 (1) As, soon (2) had, before [when]
(3) unless, to (4) louder, so
(5) so, slowly (6) such, like

解説
3 (4) so that ～ can [will / may] ...「～が…で
きる[する／である]ように」
(6) feel like ～ ing「～したい気がする」

4 (1) As it is getting dark
(2) He is relied on because
(3) He arrived after you had
(4) Even if they invite me
(5) in the front so that
(6) in such a hurry that

STEP 3　まとめ問題

1 (1)① the piano for two hours before
[when] we had lunch.
② after we had played the piano for
two hours.
(2)① she is young, she is relied on by
everyone.
② (例 1) relied on by everyone though
she is young.
(例 2) young but (she is) relied on
by everyone.
(3)① that novel twice because [as / since]
it was very interesting.
② (例 1) novel was so interesting that
I read it twice.
(例 2) was such an interesting novel
that I read it twice.
2 (1) As soon as the mother stood up, her
baby began to
(2) will be put off until it stops raining.
(3) (例 1) is so shy that he doesn't speak
unless he is spoken to.
(例 2) is so shy that he doesn't speak

if he is not spoken to.
(例 3) is such a shy boy that he doesn't
speak unless he is spoken to.
(例 4) is such a shy boy that he doesn't
speak if he is not spoken to.
(4) (例 1) practiced hard so that she
could [might / would] win the next
tennis match.
(例 2) practiced hard (in order) to
win the next tennis match.
3 (例) I'm going to recommend the
amusement park to you. I think
it's the best place because you can
enjoy a lot of attractions there. You
will never forget the beautiful view
of Mt. Fuji from the Ferris wheel.
Though the ticket is expensive, you
won't regret paying for it. You can
have fun even if you have to stand
in a long line. It will be the time
when you can enjoy talking. (Why
don't you go there?)

LISTENING

(1) we had a very good time when we went
to the aquarium last month
(2) I want to go to the art museum because
(3) We can have fun even if it rains
(4) we can go to the cafeteria in the art
museum if we need a break

1年の総合問題　　　　　　(pp.88-93)

第1回　LESSON 1 ～ 5

1 (1) went　　(2) will visit
　(3) is respected　　(4) have learned
　(5) come　　(6) boils　　(7) in
　(8) had　　(9) making
　(10) will be built

解説
1 (6) 不変の真理（例：太陽が東から登る）なので現在形で表す。
　(8) 過去のある時点（私たちが来たとき）ですでに済んでいることや，過去よりさらに以前のことは過去完了形で表す。

2 (1) How many times have you played golf until now?
　(2) I don't have to get up early today.
　(3) He was doing his homework when I called him.
　(4) We were surprised at the news.
　(5) I have known him for two years.
　(6) He is able to speak five languages.
　(7) This dictionary is made use of by many students.
　(8) He had never been to America before he became an adult.

解説
2 (3) 過去のある時点（私が彼に電話したとき）の動作を表すので，過去進行形になる。
　(4) be surprised at ～「～に驚く」
　(7) make use of ～「～を利用する」受動態は be made use of (by ～)となる。

3 (1) It was snowing in Tokyo then [at that time].
　(2) Will he stay home next Sunday?
　(3) You must not [mustn't] tell us a lie.

解説
3 (3) must not(mustn't) は「～してはいけない」という意味。

4 (1) I have been waiting for him since
　(2) More experts should be included
　(3) I spent more money than I had

解説
4 (1) 現在完了進行形は過去のある時点(this morning)から現在までずっと続いている動作を表す。

5 (1) Many children are taken care of by her.
　(2) The room was comfortable because we had just cleaned it.

解説
5 (1) take care of ～「～を世話する」受動態は be taken care of (by ～)となる。

第2回　LESSON 6 ～ 10

1 (1) more, interesting, than
　(2) as, busy, as　　(3) like, watching
　(4) to, eat　　(5) running, boy
　(6) most, of

解説
1 (4) something to eat「食べるためのもの（食べ物）」
　(6) ＜最上級＋ of the 数字・複数を表す語句 … ＞「…の中でもっとも～である」

2 (1) three times as large as ours
　(2) in order not to be late
　(3) many works painted by famous artists
　(4) It is necessary for him to
　(5) good enough to live abroad
　(6) Who plays the piano the best

解説

2(1) <three times as＋形容詞・副詞＋as ... >
「…の３倍〜である」

(3) 分詞を含む２語以上の語句で名詞を修飾する場合，名詞の後に置く。

(5) 〜 enough to ...「…できるほど十分〜だ」

(6) well(上手に)の最上級は the best。

3(1) The older we get, the weaker our memory becomes.

(2) Enjoy traveling abroad as much as possible.

(3) This coffee is too hot to drink.

解説

3(1) < The 比較級〜，the 比較級 ... >「〜であればあるほど，…だ」

4(1) natural for them to be tired

(2) how to become [be] a lawyer

(3) I heard someone singing a song

解説

4(1) < find it 〜 for 人 to ... >「人が…するのは〜だとわかる(思う)」

5(1) It is no use asking me something difficult.

(2) I like math better than any other subject.

解説

5(1) It is no use 〜 ing「〜しても無駄だ」

(2) <比較級 〜 than any other 名詞の単数形…>「ほかのどの…よりも〜だ」

第３回 LESSON 11 〜 14

1(1) which [that], has　　(2) where

(3) as, if, were　　(4) until

(5) whom [who]　　(6) That's, why

解説

1(3) as if 〜「まるで〜であるか(あったか)の

ように」as if の後は現在のことであれば過去形(be 動詞は主語に関わらず were)，過去のことであれば過去完了形となる。

2(1) would have taken you there

(2) since I have another appointment

(3) What is the most important

(4) the way he teaches English

(5) wish I had received the job offer

(6) Though I know you are busy

解説

2(4) the way S + V「S が V する方法」

3(1) Is this the village where you grew up?

(2) This book is so big that I can't put it in [into] my bag.

(3) As soon as he got off the train, he took a taxi.

解説

3(2) < so 〜 that ... >「とても〜なので…」

4(1) If I were you, I would not [wouldn't] pay attention to

(2) Unless you hurry [you are in a hurry]

(3) He is such a great actor that

解説

4(3) <such (a)＋形容詞〜＋名詞(A) that ... >「とても〜な A なので…」

5(1) Write in large letters so that we can see them.

(2) He came at seven, when we started the party.

解説

5(1) so that S 〜「S が〜するように(ために)」

(2) 関係副詞 when の非制限用法は時間について補足的に説明するのに使う。ここでは，when = and then。

APPLAUSE
ENGLISH LOGIC AND EXPRESSION I
Workbook
解答・解説

開隆堂出版株式会社
東京都文京区向丘 1-13-1

BD

4 次の４つの項目を入れて，友だち(カズ)からもらったアドバイスを英語で発表しましょう。

① この前のサッカーの試合中にオウンゴールを入れてしまった(scored on my own team)ことを悔やんでいる

② カズにアドバイスを頼むと，彼は「僕が君ならもっと懸命に練習するためにそのことを決して忘れない。でも僕が君ならあまり心配し過ぎない。君が半年前よりずっと上手いディフェンダー(defender)だと知っているから」と言ってくれた

③ カズからアドバイスをもらわなかったら僕はあきらめていただろう

④ チームで一番のディフェンダーになるために全力を尽くすつもりだ

_____

_____

_____

_____

_____

_____

🔊 LISTENING

会話を聞いて，(1)〜(4)の内容を書きとりましょう。

エイミーはスマートフォンで何かを懸命に調べています。(A: Amy　R: Ron)

A: Hmm....

R: What's wrong, Amy? Are you OK? You look frustrated.

A: Nothing serious. I'm OK.

R: But (1)_____, aren't you? Come on, Amy.

A: You know, I really miss Australian food. (2)_____! It's too expensive to order them in a restaurant. (3)_____ myself....

R: Amy, don't worry. (4)_____!

(1) _____

(2) _____

(3) _____

(4) _____

LESSON 14

接続詞

教科書 pp.110-115

STEP 1 基本問題

❶ 時を表す接続詞

1 日本語に合うように，（　　）内の接続詞を使って 2 つの英文を 1 文にしましょう。

(1) 彼女が 11 歳のときに，彼女の家族は大阪に引っ越しました。（when）

She was eleven years old. / Her family moved to Osaka.

_____

(2) 彼女の夫は夕飯を食べる前に入浴しました。（before）

Her husband took a bath. / Her husband had supper.

_____

(3) 私は宿題を終えてからゲームをするつもりです。（after）

I will finish my homework. / I will play the video game.

_____

2 次の英文を日本語に訳しましょう。

(1) Let's kill time here until it stops raining.　　　　　　注：kill time　暇をつぶす

_____

(2) As soon as he saw a policeman, he ran away.

_____

❷ 原因・理由を表す接続詞

1 日本語に合うように，（　　）内の接続詞を使って 2 つの英文を 1 文にしましょう。

(1) 弟は病気だったので，学校を休みました。（because）

My brother was ill. / My brother was absent from school.

_____

(2) キャプテンは努力家なので，私たちは彼女を尊敬しています。（as）

Our captain is a hardworking person. / We respect our captain.

_____

2 次の英文を日本語に訳しましょう。

Since you have a high fever, you shouldn't go out today.

_____

❸ 条件・譲歩を表す接続詞

1　日本語に合うように，（　　）内の接続詞を使って2つの英文を1文にしましょう。

(1) もし明日雨が降るなら，私は家にいます。(if)

It will rain tomorrow. / I will stay at home.

_____

(2) 父はひどく疲れていましたが，仕事を続けました。(though)

My father was very tired. / My father went on working.

_____

2　次の英文を日本語に訳しましょう。

(1) You should buy it even if it is expensive.

_____

(2) Unless it's an emergency, you must not press this button.

_____

❹ 目的・結果を表す接続詞

1　日本語に合うように，（　　）内の接続詞を使って2つの英文を1文にしましょう。

(1) 彼はとても早口だったので，私は彼の言うことを理解できませんでした。(so ～ that)

He spoke very fast. / I couldn't understand him.

_____

(2) それはとてもよい映画だったので，私は2回見ました。(such ～ that)

It was a very good movie. / I saw it twice.

_____

(3) 電車に間に合うように，もう出発しましょう。(so that)

Let's leave now. / We can catch the train.

_____

2　次の英文を日本語に訳しましょう。

(1) These days she is so busy that she has no time to read.

_____

(2) Please open the door so that the cat can go out.

_____

接続詞

STEP 2 実践問題

1 (　　)内から適切な語句を選びましょう。

(1) The weather forecast says (so that / that) it'll be sunny tomorrow.

(2) (Because / As soon as) we arrived there, it began to snow.

(3) We will wait here (before / until) they come.

(4) I had done my homework (because / before) they came.

(5) We have known each other (because / since) we were kids.

(6) She was angry (because / so that) I broke my promise.

(7) (Since / Though) you are so busy now, we can't invite you to the party.

(8) The tennis match will be put off (if / unless) it is rainy.

(9) The softball game will be played (if / unless) it is rainy.

(10) (But / Though) he is very shy, we respect him.

(11) The box was (so / such) heavy that she couldn't carry it.

(12) He told us (so / such) a funny story that we all laughed out loud.

(13) He worked hard (after / so that) he could support his family.

2 例にならって下線部の誤りを訂正し，文全体を書き直しましょう。

(例) My father always <u>keep my</u> promise. → My father always keeps his promise.

(1) He got up <u>until</u> the sun rose.

_____

(2) I will come back before it <u>will get</u> dark.

_____

(3) If my father <u>will cook</u> dinner, I will help him.

_____

(4) I'll buy it <u>unless</u> it is not very expensive.

_____

(5) <u>Because</u> he is not very tall, he is a good basketball player.

_____

(6) I was <u>exciting</u> so that I could not sleep last night.

_____

(7) It rained <u>such heavy</u> that they gave up playing golf.

_____

3 日本語に合う英文になるように，空所に適切な語を入れましょう。

(1) 私たちが家を出たとたんに雨が降り始めました。

_____ _____ as we left home, it began to rain.

(2) 昨夜は1時間勉強してから寝ました。

I _____ studied for an hour _____ I went to bed last night.

(3) その内気な男子は，話しかけられなければ自分からは話しません。

The shy boy does not speak _____ he is spoken _____.

(4) 私たちに聞こえるようにもっと大きな声で話してください。

Talk _____ _____ that we can hear you.

(5) その人はとてもゆっくり歩いたので，子どもたちはついていくことができました。

The man walked _____ _____ that the children could follow him.

(6) とても天気のよい日だったので，私はピクニックに行きたい気分でした。

It was _____ a nice day that I felt _____ going on a picnic.

4 日本語の意味に合うように，（　　）内の語を並べかえましょう。

(1) 暗くなりかけているので，もうおいとましなくてはなりません。

(dark / is / as / getting / it), I have to leave now.

_____

(2) 彼は面倒見がよいので頼られています。

(on / because / is / he / relied) he is very caring.

_____

(3) 君が帰ったあとで彼が到着しました。

(had / you / he / after / arrived) left.

_____

(4) たとえ彼らから招待されても，私はそのパーティーに行きません。

(me / if / invite / they / even), I won't go to the party.

_____

(5) スクリーンがよく見えるように前に座りましょう。

Let's sit (that / front / in / so / the) we can see the screen well.

_____

(6) 私はとても急いでいたので，ドアに鍵をかけ忘れました。

I was (a / that / such / hurry / in) I forgot to lock the door.

_____

LESSON 14

接続詞

STEP 3 まとめ問題

1 日本語に合うように，それぞれの書き出しに続けて英文を完成させましょう。

(1) 私たちは2時間ピアノを弾いてからお昼ごはんを食べました。

① We had played _____

② We had lunch _____

(2) 彼女は若いけれど，みんなに頼られています。

① Though _____

② She is _____

(3) あの小説はとてもおもしろかったので私は二度読みました。

① I read _____

② That _____

2 日本語に合うように，英文を完成させましょう。

(1) 母親が立ち上がると赤ちゃんが泣きだしました。

_____ cry.

(2) 運動会 (the athletic meet) は雨がやむまで延期されるでしょう。

The athletic meet _____

(3) 私の弟はとても内気なので，話しかけられなければ自分からは話しません。

My brother _____

(4) 私の妹は次のテニスの試合に勝てるように，懸命に練習しました。

My sister _____

3 次の５つの項目を入れて，春休みに行く場所を留学生に英語ですすめましょう。

① 遊園地をすすめる
② たくさんのアトラクションを楽しめるから最高の場所だと思う
③ 観覧車(the Ferris wheel)からの富士山の美しい景色を忘れることはないだろう
④ チケットは高価だが，それに支払うのを悔やむことはないだろう
⑤ 長い列に並ばなくてはならないとしても楽しむことはできる。それはおしゃべりを楽しむ時間になるだろう

_____
_____
_____
_____
_____
_____
_____

🔊 LISTENING

会話を聞いて，(1)〜(4)の内容を書きとりましょう。

ロンと華が一緒に出かける場所について話しています。(*R*: Ron　*H*: Hana)

R: Hana, where do you feel like going tomorrow?

H: Well, (1)_____. How about the zoo?

R: I really want to go there too. But the weather forecast says that it'll rain tomorrow.

H: Oh, no. Then (2)_____ the Buddha statue exhibition sounds good.

R: Good idea! (3)_____, and (4)_____.

H: Let's leave home early, so we don't have to wait in line.

(1) _____

(2) _____

(3) _____

(4) _____

1年の総合問題

第1回　LESSON1 〜 5

1 (　　)内から適切な語句を選びましょう。

(1) He (goes / went) abroad when he was a high school student.

(2) We (visit / will visit) Hokkaido next month.

(3) The man (is respected / respects) by many people.

(4) I (have learned / learn) Japanese for two years.

(5) He may (come / comes) late in the afternoon.

(6) Water (boil / boils) at 100℃.

(7) He is interested (by / in) the culture of the country.

(8) She (had / has) already finished her work when we came.

(9) What is he (make / making) now?

(10) The new school (will build / will be built) next year.

2 例にならって下線部の誤りを訂正し，文全体を書き直しましょう。

(例) My father always keep my promise. → My father always keeps his promise.

(1) How many times do you play golf until now?

_____

(2) I don't must get up early today.

_____

(3) He is doing his homework when I called him.

_____

(4) We surprised at the news.

_____

(5) I knew him for two years.

_____

(6) He is able of speaking five languages.

_____

(7) This dictionary is made use by many students.

_____

(8) He has never been to America before he became an adult.

_____

3 （　　　）内に与えられた語を必要なら形を変えて使い，英文を完成させましょう。

(1) そのとき，東京では雪が降っていました。(snow)

_____

(2) 次の日曜日，彼は家にいますか。(will / stay)

_____

(3) あなたは私たちに嘘を言ってはいけません。(must / tell)

_____

4 指示に従い，日本語に合うように，英文を完成させましょう。

(1) 私は今朝からずっと彼を待ち続けています。(現在完了進行形を使って)

_____ this morning.

(2) もっと多くの専門家(experts)をそのグループに加えるべきです。

(include を使った受動態に)

_____ in the group.

(3) 私は思っていたより多くのお金を使いました。(spend を必要なら形を変えて使って)

_____ expected.

5 次の日本語を英語に直しましょう。

(1) 多くの子どもたちが彼女の世話になっています。

_____

(2) その部屋は私たちが掃除したばかりなので，快適でした。

_____

1年の総合問題
第2回　LESSON6 ～ 10

1 日本語に合う英文になるように，空所に適切な語を入れましょう。

(1) あれよりこっちの本のほうがおもしろいです。

This book is _____ _____ _____ that one.

(2) 彼はリンダほど忙しくありません。

He is not _____ _____ _____ Linda.

(3) 私は夜遅くにスマートフォンで動画を見るのが好きです。

I _____ _____ videos with my smartphone late at night.

(4) 冷蔵庫に明日食べるものがありますか。

Is there anything _____ _____ tomorrow in the fridge?

(5) 私は走っている男の子とぶつかりそうになりました。

I almost ran into a _____ _____.

(6) この絵が5枚の中でいちばん美しいです。

This picture is the _____ beautiful _____ the five.

2 日本語の意味に合うように，(　　)内の語句を並べかえましょう。

(1) あの町は私たちの町の3倍の広さです。

That city is (large / as / ours / as / times / three).

_____

(2) 遅れないように早く出発してください。

Leave early (not / late / order / be / to / in).

_____

(3) その美術館には有名な画家が描いた作品がたくさんあります。

The museum has (famous / works / by / artists / many / painted).

_____

(4) 彼はそれを私たちに説明する必要があります。

(is / to / him / it / for / necessary) explain it to us.

_____

(5) 彼女は海外で暮らすには十分英語が上手です。

Her English is (live / to / good / abroad / enough).

_____

(6) 私たちの学校でだれがいちばんピアノが上手ですか。

(the piano / plays / best / who / the) in our school?

_____

3 (　　)内に与えられた語を必要なら形を変えて使い，英文を完成させましょう。

(1) 私たちは年を取れば取るほど，記憶力が弱くなります。(old / weak)

_____

(2) 海外旅行を存分に(できる限り)楽しんでください。(much)

_____

(3) このコーヒーは熱すぎて飲めません。(hot / to drink)

_____

4 指示があればそれに従い，日本語に合うように，英文を完成させましょう。

(1) 私は彼らが長時間労働で疲れているのは当たり前だと思いました。

I found it _____ from long hours of work.

(2) 弁護士になる方法に関する情報をインターネットで探してください。(how を使って)

Look for information about _____ on the Internet.

(3) 私は一瞬，だれかが歌を歌っているのを聞きました。

_____ for a moment.

5 次の日本語を英語に直しましょう。

(1) 私に難しい事をたずねても無駄です。

_____

(2) 私はほかのどの教科よりも数学が好きです。

_____

1年の総合問題
第3回　LESSON11 ～ 14

1 日本語に合う英文になるように，空所に適切な語を入れましょう。

(1) 私は多くの機能があるスマートフォンが欲しいです。

I want the smartphone ＿＿＿＿＿＿ ＿＿＿＿＿＿ many functions.

(2) 私は自分のお店を持つのによい場所を見つけました。

I found a good location ＿＿＿＿＿＿ I can have my own shop.

(3) 彼はまるで自分の上司のように私に話しかけます。

He speaks to me ＿＿＿＿＿＿ ＿＿＿＿＿＿ he ＿＿＿＿＿＿ my boss.

(4) 私がそれを書き終わるまで，ここで待ってもらえますか。

Please wait here ＿＿＿＿＿＿ I finish writing it.

(5) あなたが質問をした人は専門家ではありません。

The person ＿＿＿＿＿＿ you asked a question isn't an expert.

(6) 私は普段，よく歯を磨きません。そういうわけで，私は歯が悪いのです。

I usually don't brush my teeth. ＿＿＿＿＿＿ ＿＿＿＿＿＿ my teeth are bad.

2 日本語の意味に合うように，（　　　）内の語句を並べかえましょう。

(1) あなたがもう1日滞在していたら，私はそこへ連れて行ったのに。

If you had stayed for one more day, I (you / have / there / would / taken).

＿＿＿＿＿＿＿＿＿＿＿＿＿＿＿＿＿＿＿＿＿＿＿＿＿＿＿＿＿＿＿＿＿＿＿＿＿

(2) 私は今日，別に約束があるので，明日，来ていただけますか。

Please come tomorrow (I / appointment / have / another / since) today.

＿＿＿＿＿＿＿＿＿＿＿＿＿＿＿＿＿＿＿＿＿＿＿＿＿＿＿＿＿＿＿＿＿＿＿＿＿

(3) 私にとってもっとも重要なことは，他者に対する理解です。

(most / what / the / important / is) for me is understanding toward others.

＿＿＿＿＿＿＿＿＿＿＿＿＿＿＿＿＿＿＿＿＿＿＿＿＿＿＿＿＿＿＿＿＿＿＿＿＿

(4) 私たちは彼の英語の教え方を見習いたいです。

We want to learn from (he / the / English / teaches / way).

＿＿＿＿＿＿＿＿＿＿＿＿＿＿＿＿＿＿＿＿＿＿＿＿＿＿＿＿＿＿＿＿＿＿＿＿＿

(5) 私はその仕事の申し出を受けていればよかったのに。

I (had / the job offer / wish / I / received).

＿＿＿＿＿＿＿＿＿＿＿＿＿＿＿＿＿＿＿＿＿＿＿＿＿＿＿＿＿＿＿＿＿＿＿＿＿

(6) あなたが忙しいのはわかっていますが，頼みを聞いていただけますか。

(you / I / though / busy / know / are), would you do me a favor?

＿＿＿＿＿＿＿＿＿＿＿＿＿＿＿＿＿＿＿＿＿＿＿＿＿＿＿＿＿＿＿＿＿＿＿＿＿

3 (　　　)内に与えられた語を必要なら形を変えて使い，英文を完成させましょう。

(1) ここがあなたが育った村ですか。(where)

_____

(2) この本はとても大きくて，私は自分のバッグに入れることができません。(so / that)

_____

(3) 彼は列車を降りるとすぐに，タクシーに乗りました。(soon)

_____

4 指示があればそれに従い，日本語に合うように，英文を完成させましょう。

(1) 私があなたなら，そんな細かいことに注意を払わないでしょう。

_____ such a small thing.

(2) 急がなければ，コンサートに間に合いませんよ。(unless を使って)

_____, you will miss the concert.

(3) 彼はとても素晴らしい俳優なので，多くのテレビドラマに出演します。

_____ he appears in many TV dramas.

5 次の日本語を英語に直しましょう。

(1) 私たちが見えるように大きな字で書いてください。(so that を使って)

_____

(2) 彼は7時に来て，それから私たちはパーティーを始めました。

(関係副詞 when の非制限用法を使って)

_____

不規則動詞変化表

原形	現在形	過去形	過去分詞形	～ing 形
be	am / is / are	was / were	been	being
bear	bear(s)	bore	born[borne]	bearing
become	become(s)	became	become	becoming
begin	begin(s)	began	begun	beginning
break	break(s)	broke	broken	breaking
bring	bring(s)	brought	brought	bringing
build	build(s)	built	built	building
burn	burn(s)	burned[burnt]	burned[burnt]	burning
buy	buy(s)	bought	bought	buying
catch	catch(es)	caught	caught	catching
choose	choose(s)	chose	chosen	choosing
come	come(s)	came	come	coming
cost	cost(s)	cost	cost	costing
creep	creep(s)	crept	crept	creeping
cut	cut(s)	cut	cut	cutting
deal	deal(s)	dealt	dealt	dealing
do	do(es)	did	done	doing
draw	draw(s)	drew	drawn	drawing
dream	dream(s)	dreamed[dreamt]	dreamed[dreamt]	dreaming
drink	drink(s)	drank	drunk	drinking
drive	drive(s)	drove	driven	driving
eat	eat(s)	ate	eaten	eating
feel	feel(s)	felt	felt	feeling
fight	fight(s)	fought	fought	fighting
find	find(s)	found	found	finding
fit	fit(s)	fit[fitted]	fit[fitted]	fitting
fly	fly / flies	flew	flown	flying
forget	forget(s)	forgot	forgot[forgotten]	forgetting
forgive	forgive(s)	forgave	forgiven	forgiving
get	get(s)	got	got[gotten]	getting
give	give(s)	gave	given	giving
go	go(es)	went	gone	going
grind	grind(s)	ground	ground	grinding
grow	grow(s)	grew	grown	growing
hang	hang(s)	hung[hanged]	hung[hanged]	hanging
have	have / has	had	had	having
hear	hear(s)	heard	heard	hearing
hide	hide(s)	hid	hidden[hid]	hiding
hit	hit(s)	hit	hit	hitting
hold	hold(s)	held	held	holding
hurt	hurt(s)	hurt	hurt	hurting
keep	keep(s)	kept	kept	keeping
know	know(s)	knew	known	knowing

原形	現在形	過去形	過去分詞形	〜ing 形
lead	lead(s)	led	led	leading
learn	learn(s)	learned[learnt]	learned[learnt]	learning
leave	leave(s)	left	left	leaving
lend	lend(s)	lent	lent	lending
let	let(s)	let	let	letting
lie(横になる)	lie(s)	lay	lain	lying
light	light(s)	lighted[lit]	lighted[lit]	lighting
lose	lose(s)	lost	lost	losing
make	make(s)	made	made	making
mean	mean(s)	meant	meant	meaning
meet	meet(s)	met	met	meeting
melt	melt(s)	melted	melted	melting
mistake	mistake(s)	mistook	mistaken	mistaking
overcome	overcome(s)	overcame	overcome	overcoming
put	put(s)	put	put	putting
read	read(s)	read	read	reading
ride	ride(s)	rode	ridden	riding
ring	ring(s)	rang	rung	ringing
rise	rise(s)	rose	risen	rising
run	run(s)	ran	run	running
say	say(s)	said	said	saying
see	see(s)	saw	seen	seeing
sell	sell(s)	sold	sold	selling
send	send(s)	sent	sent	sending
set	set(s)	set	set	setting
shake	shake(s)	shook	shaken	shaking
shoot	shoot(s)	shot	shot	shooting
show	show(s)	showed	shown[showed]	showing
sing	sing(s)	sang	sung	singing
sink	sink(s)	sank[sunk]	sunk[sunken]	sinking
sit	sit(s)	sat	sat	sitting
sleep	sleep(s)	slept	slept	sleeping
speak	speak(s)	spoke	spoken	speaking
spend	spend(s)	spent	spent	spending
spit	spit(s)	spit[spat]	spit[spat]	spitting
stand	stand(s)	stood	stood	standing
swim	swim(s)	swam	swum	swimming
take	take(s)	took	taken	taking
teach	teach(es)	taught	taught	teaching
tell	tell(s)	told	told	telling
think	think(s)	thought	thought	thinking
throw	throw(s)	threw	thrown	throwing
understand	understand(s)	understood	understood	understanding
wake	wake(s)	woke[waked]	woken[waked, woke]	waking
wear	wear(s)	wore	worn	wearing
win	win(s)	won	won	winning
write	write(s)	wrote	written	writing

形容詞・副詞比較変化表

❶ -er / -est をつける語

原級	比較級	最上級	意味	原級	比較級	最上級	意味
big	bigger	biggest	大きい	kind	kinder	kindest	親切な
bright	brighter	brightest	明るい	large	larger	largest	大きい
busy	busier	busiest	忙しい	late	later	latest	遅れた
clean	cleaner	cleanest	きれいな	light	lighter	lightest	明るい
cold	colder	coldest	寒い	long	longer	longest	長い
cool	cooler	coolest	かっこいい	loud	louder	loudest	(音・声が)大きな
cute	cuter	cutest	かわいい	new	newer	newest	新しい
early	earlier	earliest	早い, 早く	nice	nicer	nicest	よい
easy	easier	easiest	やさしい	old	older	oldest	古い
fast	faster	fastest	速い, 速く	safe	safer	safest	安全な
great	greater	greatest	すばらしい	short	shorter	shortest	短い
happy	happier	happiest	幸福な	small	smaller	smallest	小さい
hard	harder	hardest	一生懸命に	soon	sooner	soonest	すぐに
heavy	heavier	heaviest	重い	strong	stronger	strongest	強い
high	higher	highest	高い, 高く	tall	taller	tallest	背の高い
hot	hotter	hottest	熱い, 暑い	warm	warmer	warmest	暖かい, 温かい

❷ more / most をつける語

原級	比較級	最上級	意味
beautiful	more beautiful	most beautiful	美しい
careful	more careful	most careful	注意深い
dangerous	more dangerous	most dangerous	危険な
difficult	more difficult	most difficult	難しい
easily	more easily	most easily	たやすく
exciting	more exciting	most exciting	わくわくさせるような
expensive	more expensive	most expensive	高価な
famous	more famous	most famous	有名な
helpful	more helpful	most helpful	役に立つ
important	more important	most important	重要な
interesting	more interesting	most interesting	おもしろい
popular	more popular	most popular	人気のある
useful	more useful	most useful	役に立つ
wonderful	more wonderful	most wonderful	すばらしい

❸ 不規則変化をする語

原級	比較級	最上級	意味	原級	比較級	最上級	意味
bad	worse	worst	悪い	little	less	least	少ない, 小さい
good	better	best	よい	many	more	most	(数が)たくさんの
well	better	best	上手に	much	more	most	(量が)たくさんの